ROUSING CREATIVITY

Think New Now!

by Floyd Hurt

CRISP
PUBLICATIONS

ROUSING CREATIVITY

Think New Now!

CREDITS

Editor: George Young

Cover & Interior Design: Fifth Street Design, Berkeley CA

Cover & Interior Art: Mike Powers

© 1999 by Floyd Hurt

Printed in the United States of America by Bawden Printing Company

www.crisp-pub.com

Distribution to the U.S. Book Trade

National Book Network
4720 Boston Way
Lanham, MD 20706

800/462-6420

99 00 01 02 10 9 8 7 6 5 4 3 2 1

Library of Congress Catalog Card Number 99-70552

Hurt, Floyd

Rousing Creativity

ISBN 1-56052-547-9

Additional publications, products, services offered by Floyd Hurt & Associates:

Rousing Creativity keynote addresses
Rousing Creativity workshops
Rousing Creativity Quarterly Newsletter
Rousing Creativity Assessments and Consulting
Customized Articles for Your Publication
Think New Now! audio tape

Home Page: www.rousingcreativity.com

PART 5 / The Game   71

PART 6 / Walking the Walk: Taking Action   101

Epilogue

Appendix A / Sample Sessions

Appendix B / The Worksheet Bank

Appendix C / A creativity Reading List

Acknowledgments

An opus like Rousing Creativity is never the work of one person. It is a birthing process taking a host of mid-wives. Each mid-wife comes in his/her own particular form of questioner, editor, poker, no-sayer, prodder, yea-sayer, philosopher, and critic. My deep thanks and appreciation to each and every one is indeed small compensation for all their input and help. It is, however, a start and as the opportunity arises, I will do all I can to repay the debt.

With this in mind, I would like to give special thanks to a few folks who were on the ride through the thick and the thin. They deserve a medal of some sort.

Jim Henerberry. I have no idea where Jim gets his perseverance, patience, and talent but these have been the essential forces which drove this project to the end point. Jim has a very nasty habit of not letting things slip through the cracks . . .a talent I try very hard to leech out of him. To no avail. That's the reason things get done. My special thanks to my associate and friend.

Lynn Merhib. Look in the dictionary under talent, drive, and support and you'll find a glossy 8 x 10 of Lynn. On a personal and professional level Lynn is more than a special person; she's a mythological figure. As the VP of Probe, Inc. (an advertising agency we own) she has taken the company to a height causing nose bleeds. While most of us are looking for a pencil, Lynn has remembered everything, assigned tasks, and is at work on the project. If I could just learn how she does it, I would triple my productivity.

Mike Powers. The most creative guy I have ever known. Give Mike a sentence, you'll get a concept. The illustrations in this book are his. In all my years in the "creative" business I have seldom seen anyone with his drive to find new ways to communicate ideas. Nor have I known anyone so willing to risk new thinking and to build on others' thoughts or wild ideas without worrying about who gets credit. This is a rare talent indeed and if you find it in your organization, chain that person to the wall, feed'um, but never never let him/her go.

Joel Smith. The philosopher, computer guy, astronomer, kayaking buddy. Everyone in my life knows more than I. But, on very rare occasions I have actually fooled people into thinking I have a small insight. Joel, I can never fool. Damn! Because of this he has been a most reliable sounding board on every new concept that enters my head. We don't always agree, but we do clarify points in an open and productive setting. You should hope for such a person in your life.

The rest of the list is longer . . . far too long to ever do it justice.

There is, however, a dedication.

With that, I dedicate this book to my mother, Laurie Hurt. Not only is she a terrific person, but she's an outstanding mom. Thanks for the start, the push, and helping make my journey a joy. Where did I ever find you?

Welcome

Thanks for trusting me with your time.

What you learn from this book is entirely up to you. It can push you and offer challenges, but when you put it down and go back to work, you'll be dealing with the same problems—the same faces. Your world will have retained its old mind-sets and those around you won't truly be interested in what you've learned.

Your charge: stick with it and usher in new ideas and new challenges. It will be tough. The raging tide of the status quo is a running, thundering tide of self-perpetuation. To alter it even a little takes guts, stamina, and a determined sense of who you are. There'll be bullets to dodge—so what. Isn't that better than sitting at the grey center of the merry-go-round watching the brass rings flash by in a vanishing world of "maybe next time?" There is no "next time." There is only here and now . . . and you.

This book has two objectives:

To make you think!
To make you act!

If this is not achieved, we all lose. To help achieve these objectives, continually ask yourself these questions:

- **Am I being challenged?**

- **Am I giving my full attention?**

- **Am I looking for applications in my life and work?**

- **Do I understand that learning is my responsibility, all mine?**

- **Will I let somebody or some "situation" hold me back?**

and at the end of your reading:

- **What have I gained and how will I put it to use?**

You'll quickly notice several features of this book designed to help you make it work for you.

- First are the worksheets. They are intended to be copied and used. Do so and reap the creative rewards.

- Second is "The Game." Use it to break into uncharted territory.

- Third are my phone number 1 (800) THINK NU and home page (www.rousingcreativity.com). Use these to continue your dialogue with this material, to further your education, to ask questions, to make suggestions. I welcome your input and will respond.

Let's get going . . . ENJOY!

Why Rousing Creativity?

. . . because man cannot create on motivation alone. We all love the platitudes; they feel good. "Mind over matter." "Think positively." "Can do." But platitudes don't solve problems: YOUR ACTIONS DO.

This book promises more than just another exercise in corporate cheerleading. It doesn't build you up, only to have reality knock you down. It prepares you.

It prepares you first as an individual. A prerequisite to realizing effective creativity depends on understanding and adopting some critical philosophical principles. Without this foundation any new-found creative drive will quickly atrophy and you will slip back into the comfortable, habitual patterns of your life.

Secondly, it prepares you to participate in and *lead groups* which will expand or step outside established boundaries. Without a thorough and clear understanding of the philosophy of creativity, your ability to spark new thinking will be limited indeed.

This book focuses primarily on creativity in the corporate environment. To explore it, however, with only that in mind would be to miss so many other applications of the principles and techniques. Whether you are

- **leading a team in developing a new business strategy,**

- **joining a committee to simplify order processing,**

- **discussing with a colleague ways to improve morale,**

- **attending your local PTA meeting,**

- **helping your family plan a vacation, or**

- **thinking up better ways to organize your closet**

the philosophy and techniques here can benefit you.

YES, use this book to push your business over the top. BUT don't stop there. Creativity, much more than just an effective business tool, is a way of life, a way of seeing the possibilities and opportunities in your world rather than its limitations. Use this material to find and embrace opportunities in *all* areas of your life.

Every aspect of this book is designed to make the creative process more productive and enjoyable. Read with an open disposition. Keep bias and prejudice from your mind; they will taint and limit your understanding of this material just as they will destroy any creative session. If you approach a creative session with even one small pre-conceived notion, you will restrict yourself and those around you.

Take a risk. Turn the page and make the journey. Leave that proper, corporate image and that stuffy, societal baggage at the door. Open your mind to all the options. Who knows who you will become along the way?

PART 1

The Journey to Break Point

Two Philosophical Challenges

Philosopher, Friedrich Nietzsche, presented one of the two most haunting and challenging of all philosophical propositions: *Eternal Return.*

To paraphrase: What if, one day (or one evening), you were approached by a demon who told you that you will have to live this life, that you are now living, over and over again in exact repetition, forever? You could change nothing. Not a word, not an act, not a rain drop, nothing. Everything would be the same and you would relive it over and over for eternity. What would you do? Would you throw yourself down, gnash your teeth, and curse the demon? Or, is your life of such a satisfying magnitude that you would leap for joy and bless him because you have never heard of anything more divine?

Take a second to think about these options. How would you respond? Most people would not choose to live their life over again as they have lived it.

Now look at the same general proposition, but this time in a somewhat more lenient light: Is there one time in your life that you *would* choose to live over and over? Not the whole thing, just a selected part. What is it and why would you choose that time or that event? The answer may tell you a great deal about what you value and perhaps some of the new choices you should be making.

Consider now a corollary proposition—the one that really counts: If you could construct your life, starting today, in such a manner that you would be content to live it over and over again for all eternity, how would you construct it? What would you do and in what manner would you live so you would have no compunction about reliving it innumerable times? Would you give yourself the courage to take the risks? Would you write the great novel? Would you shoot the photographs, sing the songs, make the movies, write the scripts? Would you start your own company, speak up in meetings? What would you do?

In these questions, responsibility has shifted from the demon to you. How does it feel?

Stop here—go back and read the last couple of paragraphs again. Now, take a walk and really think about this proposition. Don't keep reading and treat this challenge like just another paragraph in just another book you read and put on a shelf, hoping you have absorbed the information. You haven't. To get the most out of yourself and this book you must invest yourself in the deep consideration and repetition of these challenges. If you are reading this just to get through a book on creativity, close it and put it away. This material demands more of you.

The second provocative challenge comes from Jean-Paul Sartre, the existentialist. It is a clear and simple statement: "There are no excuses." If you happen to be one of those people who truly understands that there are no excuses, you are indeed a social deviant. Contemporary society is fraught with people living a life of excuses. "My mother was an alcoholic." "My father abused me." "My car won't start." "What would the neighbors say?" "I'm too old." "I'm male." "I'm female." "I'm black." "It's raining." There is not a single excuse, however, that can preclude you, at some level, from working toward a goal that is important to you. Not one. This does not mean there won't be things to overcome or that it won't be tough. So what? "Overcoming" is what makes life the adventure it is. If, for a nanosecond, you choose to wallow in the limitations of excuses, your eternal return will be bleak indeed and your life's adventures will be shallow. There is no excuse for not creating the kind of life you would eagerly live over and over again. If you think there is, reach for the channel changer.

Creativity has nothing to do with how well you write, how well you paint, how well you play the tuba; these are the children of creativity. True creativity is the philosophy of your life. It is a philosophy that does not yield to the vicissitudes of cultural winds. It is a philosophy that only pays passing deference to the limits of the "givens." Creativity questions everything and has no compunction about inquiring into the taboo, the unexpected, the unaccepted, and the disallowed. Above all, creativity is a philosophy of acting courageously. The creative person does not have to be a great artist, a great singer, a great sculptor. She has only to be great at acting on her desire to experience things and she will, by definition, be creative. She will also have a vastly more interesting life.

At the time of this writing, the oldest known living person is a French woman named Jeanne Louise Calment. She is 120 years old. When asked what she does now at her age, she replied, "I play back the good memories of my life."

Will you be able to say that? If not, take note and do something about it.

Seeing the Need For Creativity

"Why is there time?" a student once asked his professor.

"So everything doesn't happen at once," the professor replied.

At the end of the second millennium it seems the nature of our time is changing and everything *is* happening at once. Product life cycles once measured in years, if not decades, are now measured in months, sometimes weeks. Television programs which lasted season after season now face oblivion with a single ratings report. Individuals who used to change jobs once or twice in their working lives now compile resumes with six or seven different jobs in several different industries, all by the age of 40.

The old moorings are gone, rotted away. The new millennium will neither require nor expect moorings. It will expect change. It will demand instantaneous and innovative thinking at all levels. It will ask us to be more and more creative in how we do things and how we live our lives. It will tolerate nothing less.

New products, new procedures, "just in time" distribution, and lightening fast computers on every lap have become necessities for businesses trying to get ahead, and stay ahead. In reality, though, there is no way to keep up. As soon as it's "plugged in," it's superseded. Even before a new product hits the shelf, it's been copied by the competition. As soon as a new employee is trained and up to speed, he is offered a position with another company. Making change and adapting to change are the orders of the day. Success, even mere survival, demands creative thinking. Without it, you and your organization will be trampled by the stampede into the future. It's just that simple.

For the individual trapped in this time warp, the path can be a dark sea where the buoys and channel markers are moved or removed at the whim of unseen forces. As organizations downsize, hire temporary employees, and replace finely skilled workers with computer-controlled machines, personal career goals get lost in the peaking tides. The goals and objectives of closely knit teams shift with each new meeting. Pet projects, in the works for months, are suddenly shelved with no explanation. New directions and new projects are planned with unrealistic demands, unrealistic deadlines, and unrealistic pressure. Re-action becomes the order of the day.

To keep up, the beleaguered individual turns to his computer and finds it erupting with instant information. Information that has assumed a life of its own, and in some very real way is constructing a monument to its own importance. But even here the CRT-stunned individual detects a perplexing shift. Information has become its own enemy. At the touch of a key, the computer spews out facts and figures in obscene torrents. Information looses its importance in direct proportion to its volume. Information becomes a commodity and the "Information Age" trivializes itself with its own mass. More storage, bigger screens, faster processors become an end unto themselves, and the real reason for accumulating the information becomes less and less important, and more and more unclear. What are we left with besides information, information, information?

At the epicenter of this revolution is a shadowy figure, "*the emerging individual.*" The emerging individual realizes that if she has access to all this information, everyone else does too. If she can retrieve it all at the speed of light, everyone else can too. The emerging individual understands that it is not the information that matters, but what is done with it that counts. The emerging individual knows the brass ring will not go to the person with the most information, but to whoever uses it most creatively.

The emerging individual is unwilling to give in to society's relentless drive to make us homogeneous. He perceives the dangers associated with going against the social tide, but takes those risks anyway. He knows you don't have to please everyone, nor can you. The emerging individual believes the demeaning notion of political correctness of any kind is as stifling today as it was when George Orwell foresaw it in his novel, *1984*. This is not the field on which he wishes to play.

The emerging individual possesses a gut level awareness that there is no "collective responsibility"; there is only individual responsibility. She knows that as we pass through the gate into postmodern society we will find no mythology to guide us. The gods have all been stripped of their magnetism, mysticism, and majesty. We have been left alone as crew, navigator, and captain of our own destinies. The emerging individual embraces these challenges and is elated, not confused by the unknown.

Finally, the emerging individual sees the world as an hour glass. The sand in the top is all the knowledge and experience of the ages. It is to be tapped, assimilated, used. The bottom of the hour glass is the output of life. This output will become either building blocks for others to use, or it will be dust lost in the wind of time. The emerging individual knows that the exact center of the hour glass, the tiny neck through which the sand rushes at blinding speed, is the only real time there is in all the universe. It is here, where present and past meet, that life takes place. We either capture life here or it slips past us, gone forever.

Such is the world as we exit the second millennium and enter the third . . .

No book can prepare you for every change of your world in your time. There are too many variables. The best we can hope for is to gain insight into a new attitude that will foster growth and kill stagnation. As you work your way through this material, as you play your part on the larger stage, let one concept be your guide:

- **There are no completely right or wrong answers to anything.****

For thousands of years, people have searched for absolutes. They can't be found. They don't exist.

If you want to play in the field of creativity, open your life to chance and accidents and you'll find something amazing: a planet awash in a vast array of differences. These differences make the world a spicy, remarkable place. They offer up a smorgasbord of delights available to anyone willing to taste, and not judge what they find distasteful as bad, only different. On every level, accepting the "different" is more fun, exciting, and rewarding than guarding against the "bad." Save the word "bad" for the bullies who attack change with no understanding of it and, worse yet, no willingness to learn. Relish the rest. After all, this is your time. It won't come again. So, take the journey, embrace the risk, explore the different, and take control of your creative future.

** 2 + 2 = 4; FDR is dead: understood.

Break Point:
Taking Control of Your Creative Future

Defining creativity in all its subtlety is an impossibility.

　　The impossible should not deter.

Creativity, a working definition:

Any new action you take that causes a reaction.

Consider the breadth of this definition. There is no measure of magnitude in it. You can paint the Sistine Chapel or the back yard fence, and, if you cause a reaction, you're creative. There is no judgment of right and wrong or better and worse in it. Develop penicillin or plastique explosives and you are equally creative. There is no reference to social standards in it. "That's awful!" or "That's disgusting!" or "That's insane!" is just as creative as "That's great!" There is no time restriction in it. A reaction today is no more or less creative than a reaction a decade or a century from now.

This definition does make three demands of you:

　　1) **you must act**

　　2) **your actions must be new to you**

　　3) **your actions must cause reactions.**

To sit around and think up ideas, no matter how earth shattering, and not act on them is, by this definition, not creativity. An analogy: creative thoughts are to creativity as recipes are to eating. If you don't gather the ingredients, cook the meals, and eat them . . . you die. If you don't act on your creative thoughts, your creativity is dead.

　　Approached through the portal of this definition, the door to creativity is easily opened by anyone willing to accept the risk of acting in a new way. To anyone unwilling to risk acting or exposing their actions to the light of day, the same door is bolted shut. If this definition makes the process of creativity sound simple, it does. Moving forward with the risk of creative action is not.

Your Journey Toward Creativity

To suddenly become "creative" requires time and work, hard work. You can read every book ever written on the subject, but until you understand the journey you have taken to get where you are and the journey you must take to become more creative, you will be on the sidelines. Until you act on what you learn, you'll never be creative.

What follows is the core of this book. It demands a slow read. It demands thought and reflection. It demands understanding on a gut level or it will slip away, never becoming part of your conscious behavior.

The following four points are essential points in understanding how to achieve creativity in your life. Consider them carefully. Don't just read. This is not a speed reading contest. If you are not willing to invest your time and your mind, merge back into the herd and continue tilting at the windmill of "what could have been . . . if only?"

Point One: THROWNESS (Martin Heidegger's term)

The first fact: you were thrown into the world through no choice of your own. You were born in 1949 not 1499. You were born male or female, or white or black, or rich or poor. These are the facts of your life, and barring major surgery, there is little you can do about it.

Another fact: any physicist will tell you that by the simple addition of your energy to the universe, nothing in all of time will ever be the same. You have changed everything. Most of us fail to realize this and through some convoluted rationale prefer to view ourselves as an insignificant part of some "great unknown." How can this be if you have changed everything? Keep your worth in the only perspective that makes sense and will make you believe in your true worth.

One more fact: you are living in the most propitious of all times. Why? Because it is the only time you have and why choose to view that time as anything but propitious. An inauspicious time fits no one and is reserved for the complainers and anyone seeking an excuse or an out for their lack of action. It's your decision. Choose your time.

Point Two: EVENTS

Family, school, politics, religion, friends are the "events" that define the "givens" of the world into which you are thrown. "Events" fix on us the mythology of our terrain. We believe that our government is the right government, that our economy is the right economy, that our religion is the right religion. We become moral imperialists and insist that others embrace our values. Value rigidity sets in and we often cling to standards well past their obsolescence. "Events" fail to inform us that morality and values are correct only as a function of time and geography. If you were thrown into any other time or onto any other continent, the different "givens" of that time and place would be just as unequivocally correct as the ones you live by now.

Observe the passing of the years. All those values deemed so essential a century ago, a decade ago, a year ago, *even yesterday* change color, tone, and hue constantly. Aren't you left wondering why so much effort goes into forcing these moralities? Remember, geography and time create the "events," and "events" are *your* reality, not *the* reality.

Point Three: MIND-SET

"Events" turn into actions; actions turn into a mind-set. Our life becomes a circle where what we do locks us into a mind-set that dictates what we do. We attend classes, go to political rallies, watch TV, go to church and our minds close around those concepts like the pseudopodia of an amoeba. Through such action, our values can ossify and our tolerance for—and involvement with—things outside the amoebic membrane narrow. We act on what we know and each action strengthens our mind-set, reflecting back the image of us as we see ourselves . . . the pseudopod turns to stone.

Changing a mind-set may be the most challenging task a human being can undertake. The world in which you now move offers few new events to provide a different set of "givens." Your learning cycle is constricted by the pressing need to just get through the day. Also, through your actions you have established a mode of behavior for yourself, usually enforced by everyone around you. That mode of behavior yields understood and expected boundaries: a persona. It defines you, and it defines your relationship with people important to you. You grow to recognize yourself in the way you are treated. You begin to act within those boundaries.

If you push against those boundaries in a way that is alien to your established persona, the response is: "Why do you want to do that? You've never wanted to do that before!" Because the people around you are important to you and because your new venture is risky, you question the move, analyze the risk, focus on the "catastrophic potential" of the venture and the threat to your life as you are living it, and you retreat into the old persona, tumbling back well within the defined boundaries. Returning from each of these forays to the edge of your persona without having stepped outside your boundary, closes the boundary a little more. Soon the forays and the risks they involve become too taxing. They produce too much anxiety. Effort wanes. You have abdicated and become unwilling to push your boundaries in the face of actions that have defined you in the past. You become proscribed and slowly slide from quiet desperation to confirmed desperation. Your creative potential slips away.

You begin to resent (yourself) by projecting your anger at your confinement onto those *you* allow to limit you. You wonder why your relationship has lost its sparkle. You wonder where the novelty has gone. You peer outside the boundary and question why you can't bring new things in. You resent the fact that you let it happen and that you are now locked into a confining world that you made.

There is at this point a blinding insight: your resentment has nothing to do with people or events and what they have "done to you;" your plight, you realize, is due to your own impotence and your own acquiescence. You now see resentment in its true and self-illuminating light, a light that (no matter how hard you try to re-direct it), always focuses back on its source: you. You start to understand the absolute meaning of resentment. Reality wins and you know that you are the arbiter of all of this. You reach for the channel changer.

Creativity demands newness. It demands going out of your bounds, ferreting out new events to construct new "givens" in your life. You must then act on these new "givens" and integrate them back into your world. When you do, your life becomes an adventure of expansion, not of constriction. You find yourself on shaky ground. There is a tingle in the back of your neck as you venture out. You go. Your creativity grows. Your desperation wanes. Your resentment disappears and the prospect of your own adventure captivates you, leaving no residue of fear.

Point Four: TAKING ACTION, BREAK POINT

Welcome to *Break Point*. You have made the journey from *throwness*, to *events*, to *mind-set*. You have reached the edge, the point where you actually have to decide your next move. It is called *Break Point* because it demands a break in the motion of your thinking and actions. It usually also means a break from the way you have done things in the past.

Understanding the concept of Break Point and acting on this understanding may prove to be the most important single event in taking control of your life. Take the time to think about it and digest it from your own perspective and with your own baggage. Don't dismiss the idea without allowing time for it to grow.

In a sentence, the concept of *Break Point*:

> **"It is not *what* we decide to do, but *how* we decide it that matters."**

What this statement requires is that, at the point of significant decisions, we pause just long enough to consider *why* we would choose to make one decision as opposed to another. This pause removes the focus from the content of the specific decision to the process of arriving at a choice. It is during this pause that we are faced with two distinct routes we can take to arrive at a decision: *Facticity* or *Transcendency*.

The first route: Facticity

Facticity is a term used extensively by Jean-Paul Sartre in defining how we view *"facts"* as *"truths"* when indeed they are not truths at all but "givens." As discussed earlier, these "givens" are the result of our "events." Since "events" are so dependent upon time and place, our "givens" are almost always subject to change, if we look at their origin and validity dispassionately. The importance of this analysis is to realize that far too often we make decisions based on facticity, assuming it is the only choice available, when it is not. Decisions made in this way, according to Sartre, are made in "bad faith."

Some "givens" provide a footing that helps keep things moving along on a desired track. The key word here is "desired." Too often we think we are on a desired track, when indeed we are simply on a track that has assumed a life of its own, and we don't take the time to question the speed, direction, or validity of the ride.

A person locked into a world governed by *facticity* often becomes a spectator. Her actions lose all authenticity because they are not really her own; they are the actions expected of her by others. She finds herself buying into particular beliefs with no consideration as to where these beliefs originated, why they have any power over her, or why she should adhere to them. She moves on blind faith that a course of action is "correct" and she refuses to pose questions that challenge that course or would prove unsavory to the world in which she moves. She becomes Nietzsche's "Last Man," sitting on a couch with a blank stare as the world passes by in a dull shade of gray.

The second route: Transcendence

In a philosophical sense "transcendence" has many complex meanings. For our purposes it means going past the boundaries or limits we've set for ourselves. If a thought or action seems risky, or if it is outside our "usual" consideration or involvement, we have entered the world of *transcendence*. We have also entered the only world where creativity takes place. If you recall our definition of creativity: *"any new action you take that causes a reaction,"* it's clear that to be creative you must act outside the bounds of your "givens." It's in this novel realm that everything interesting seems to occur. It is here that we are required to reach out into the unknown and bring back something new, something that challenges us to re-evaluate where we are, who we are, what we can accomplish, and to explore the true depth of our capabilities. It is only by pursuing transcendent activities that we feel alive in the sense that *we*, ourselves, not the demands of the system, have made this move; it is *we* who must adjust to the dictates of a new environment; it is *we* who make the rules; and it is *we* who stand to win or lose. We have assumed the personal responsibility and accountability to blaze a path into this new terrain. We have become Nietzsche's Superman and it feels great to be so alive.

All this starts with a simple pause at Break Point. It is no more complicated than that. What you do during that pause, however, is indeed more complicated. You have to be truthful with yourself. You have to be willing to employ a new standard of measurement to determine whether you want to stick with the "given" or take the leap into something different. How do you do that?

We already have a couple of keys:

Eternal Return and *No Excuses.*

To employ these philosophical challenges and begin living your new creative life, at your Break Points pause, and ask yourself these key questions:

- **Which decision would I be willing to live with over and over again . . . forever?**

- **Would I be willing not to push this boundary again and again and again?**

- **Would I be willing to back away from this challenge, forever?**

- **Would I want to pull back from presenting this idea because someone thought I shouldn't, for eternity?**

- **Will I regret this decision forever?**

It takes only a few seconds to ask these questions, but the results will have a far-reaching impact on the direction your life takes.

A note of caution must be expressed here. With a clear understanding of Break Point, your actions can never be the same. With this knowledge, you will be keenly aware that you are the master of your own fate and you can't relinquish your decisions to a "Magic Helper" ever again. You have no excuses except the self-imposed. You have crossed a threshold and from here on you must decide which way to go on your own. You can't go back; you know too much.

There are a host of things that will preclude many of us from making the move into transcendence. At base, all of these revolve around a single factor:

Our willingness to take risks.

Risk is the cornerstone of creativity. Anyone willing to press on with an idea or activity, regardless of the slings and arrows, will have a more creative life and more delicious experiences. She won't always win, but to the creatively driven person, winning is not the goal. It is accepting the challenge to become the person you set out to be. It is the thrill of the journey.

Understanding the principle of Break Point is a crucially important first step in realizing your creative potential. Taking a short pause to interrupt the cycle of your "givens" will pay great rewards in the satisfaction of knowing you are now in control of your life. You may choose never to venture outside the boundaries of your current world. But won't it be satisfying to know that you have decided this and that it was not all just the caprice of habit? Besides, by constantly forcing yourself to consider the benefits of going or staying and by taking a hard look at what lay outside your boundaries, sooner or later you'll find yourself making the leap. The goal of this book is to prepare you for that moment so you'll know when it arrives and so you can make the most of it.

Achieving Creativity: The Five Essential Factors

In addition to making decisions "in good faith" at Break Point, there are five essential factors which contribute to your creative potential. By combining an understanding and acceptance of these five factors with an understanding and acceptance of the role Break Point plays in your creative process, you will find the fuel you need to power your creative future. From here on, you are in the driver's seat with only your own imagination to limit you.

The first factor:

It's your life and you are responsible for it. This is perhaps one of the most frightful notions of the late 20th century. If this concept is novel to you, or if it makes you ill at ease, then any step you take toward fruitful creativity will be into sticky mud or shifting sand. If you don't believe that you are personally and totally responsible for who you are, what you are, how you are, and where you want to go, any progress you try to make will be difficult, if not impossible. You'll claim that "everything else" keeps you from progressing. If you are waiting for the muses to visit before you undertake a creative adventure, you are leaving your destiny to mythology and the whim of make-believe. Your wait will be long, and life is short. If you spend even a second of your day simply hoping, wallowing in regret, finding excuses, or blaming others, throw this book into the sea—your destiny is elsewhere.

The second factor:

You must act on what you learn and what you think. There is no creativity until there is action. In fact, there is no you until you act. There is only a shadow. It is by your actions that you define who you are and what you become. It is by your transcendent actions (see Break Point) that you cause experiences and participate in experiences. It is by your actions that events take the specific course they do. Events don't care. They won't wait for you. They will unfold with or without you. Towering buildings will be built, emotionally packed photographs will be captured, mesmerizing concertos will be played. With you or without you. The building, the camera, the piano, they don't care. Your involvement is critical if you are to taste life.

There will of course be hurdles to jump and snares to avoid. So what? It is in the face of these hurdles and snares, and the trials they provide, that we experience life. If we seek to avoid these trials, we seek to avoid the fun and the joy of accomplishment, and we miss the opportunity to fully experience our very existence.

Never forget that a "can do" attitude never did anything. The world is full of glassy eyed people with a "can-do" attitude who *never* do. They read all the books, talk the game, and pontificate on how important that "can-do" attitude is. Not you. You don't talk the game, you play the game. You jump the hurdles. You figure out ways around the snares. You act, and in that action, you live. The rest is noise.

The third factor:

You teach people how to treat you. The statement, "Oh, you're not creative; you'll never do that," is not a fact; it is a "given," and it contains a critical bit of information. Any statement like this should evoke two questions: "What in my behavior has taught this person to think that way of me?" and "What proscription have I accepted?" It will take a formidable effort to ask those questions and not be defensive. If your actions are giving people the wrong impression, don't blame them. Look inside and determine what picture of yourself you have been presenting.

The way others treat you is always a function of how you treat yourself and without some critical self-reflection, the way others treat you soon becomes the only way you can envision and treat yourself. Let the reflection you see of yourself in others be a helpful guide to the changes you want to make. Act and watch the effect these actions have on those whose opinion you value. Those reactions will help you determine if you are on the right road. If you want to be creative, act creatively and watch the reflection.

Remember that for every action, there is an equal and opposite reaction. If you are reaching out into transcendence, there will be many people who will try to rein you back in. The pressure will be great and many people can't stand it. Can you?

The fourth factor:

The willingness, if not the passion, to change. You can't change the world. You can change you, and when you change you, you will in fact change the world. Let nothing get in your way. At the "Break

Point" of any opportunity, stop for that introspective second and think about what you are going to do. Remember, it is not what you decide to do that counts, it's how you decide. Are you basing your decision on *facticity* or *transcendence*? Are you giving in to the way you have always done it, the way you are expected to do it? Or are you taking the risk of moving in a new way, knowing you will meet resistance?

When you decide to move in a new direction, decide how you want to be and how it is different than the way you are now. Generate a clear picture of that difference in your mind. Then ask yourself, if you were that new persona, how would you talk? Now, find the words and use those words complete with inflections and gestures. What would you wear? Buy the clothes and wear them. How would you carry yourself? Carry yourself that way and your body will begin to believe that this new persona is who you are. It can't tell the difference. Lastly, what would you actually do in the guise of this new persona? Do it. Read the "new persona" books, go to the "new persona" movies, frequent the "new persona" restaurant. The second you do this, you have changed the world. You are now a person with a passion for change because you know that it is critical to the creative effort. You have found your "Break Point," and, invariably, many people you know will try to stop you!

The fifth factor:

Courage. It can be described no better than the poet Jal-al al-Din Rumi does in the first line of one of his quatrains:

> *Courage: A gazelle turns to face a pack of lions.*

Without courage, everything you would like to be, dream of doing, hope of achieving—grinds to a halt. Any step on the path to greater creativity must be a step in a new direction. It is a step that demands thinking and acting outside the norm. It means seeing the world with new eyes, listening with new ears, touching, tasting, and smelling with raw nerves that are anxious to take it all in knowing that it all passes. That takes courage.

The rest of this book is designed to encourage you to think and act in ways that may not be normal in your day-to-day life. You will be challenged to participate in groups where all eyes will be on you. It is here and now that you can decide to turn and face the lions. The second that the old "they are looking" or "I could never say that" feeling comes over you, pause for one second and ask yourself why you feel that way. Who are these people and what power have you relinquished to them to make you to feel that way? The answer will surprise and delight you.

Another Rumi poem:

> *Keep walking though there is no place to get to*
> *Don't try to see through the distances, that's not for human beings*
> *Move within, but don't move the way fear makes you move*

Creativity: *Any new action you take that causes a reaction.*

You can choose the safety of smoothly paved roads or the creative curves of unexplored territory. The journey is yours. Proceed courageously.

PART 2

Setting the Stage:

Your Role in a Creative Group/Session

Ground Rules

Several principles recur throughout this book. These are the *Ground Rules* of all effective creative enterprises. Look for them and live by them to enhance your creative output.

Ground Rule #1

Avoid judgement of any kind until the right moment. Judgements come in many shades and styles. Some constrain the judge and some squash the judged.

Value judgements, those invisible beliefs we all have about rights and wrongs or bests and worsts, often trick us into judging too early and missing the latent beauty of an idea. It takes real effort and self awareness to see around these. Some ideas will make you uncomfortable. They will push your buttons. They should. If they don't, you're staying too close to home; venture further out. And, when the discomfort comes, don't run home and hide; embrace it. How? By allowing yourself to entertain all the possibilities. Remember, no matter how wild or deviant the idea, *you don't have to do it*. You do have to push the limits and see where that pressure takes you. It takes work. If the ideas are great enough, you might even break a sweat.

Judging others is another creativity hatchet. Who in a room filled with judges will take even a calculated risk? This is one of the easiest creativity hatchets to stop. Just keep your mouth SHUT. How much good can it do right now to say "It's too expensive" or "We already tried it that way" or "That's stupid"? There will be time to weigh and judge later. Now is the time to allow and encourage anything and everything. When you feel that judgement rising in you, hold your tongue and your eyes and your head and anything else that might signal your opinion. Everyone cares and everyone will shut down if judgements start.

Ground Rule #2

Everyone is creative. By its very nature the act of living, of getting up each day and making a life, is a creative process. So, by nature every single one of us is creative. Accept this. The only difference between "creative people" and the rest of us is *"their" willingness to commit to their creativity,* to overcome the limitations imposed by others. Take some chances. And, all of a sudden you'll be one of "them," in name and action.

Ground Rule #3

Be aware of your own defenses. We can all be defensive, especially if we feel we are being attacked. It is only common sense and often a survival tactic to employ defensive strategies. In an ideal creative setting, you would never feel the need to be defensive because no one would ever attack you or your ideas. If and when someone does attack, stem your rising tide of defensiveness. Do as the skilled matador does: step aside and let the raging bull pass. With no one to fight, the "bull" will calm down and you will have given yourself, your idea, and the session that much more chance of successfully reaching your goals. It *is* worth the effort!

Ground Rule #4

Develop your passion. Passion is the spice in life. Without passion life simply sits in your mouth like a wad of moist cardboard. With a dash of passion, it becomes a delicious experience. Where does passion come from? Can it be cultivated? Passion comes from commitment. By committing ourselves to our ideas, no matter how wild, we cultivate passion. Commit and your passion will grow and become a faithful companion.

Ground Rule #5

Keep it in the room: confidentiality counts. Try this experiment. The next time a friend tells you a secret, post it on the bulletin board. Now count the days until that friend tells you another secret. For people to take the kind of risks that produce truly valuable ideas, they need to know they have the freedom to express themselves. Any suspicion that a boundary-breaking idea might get back to a less than receptive "boss" greatly reduces creative potential. Confidentiality is a must. Without it you might as well use the notes from the last session and save everyone's time.

Nothing said in a creative session leaves the room *unless everyone agrees*. If word spreads that ol' Joe said something dumb, not only will ol' Joe not come back, but neither will anyone else. Keep it classified.

Ground Rule #6

Build on other's ideas. Someone in the group will say something that sparks a new notion for you. Before you present your thought, acknowledge the original idea and indicate that you want to build on it. This kind of credit fosters a team spirit and encourages greater participation. Everyone likes to have their ideas recognized, even you.

Ground Rule #7

Keep the energy up. Stand, move, gesture, have people draw pictures. Movement generates enthusiasm and energy; energy creates energy. If everyone sits around, your session will lack the drive it needs to come up with new ideas. Move and make them move. It will pay off handsomely.

Ground Rule #8

Stick to the problem/topic. In any session, it is easy to wander off into the weeds. This trek is not always bad because it may generate unique ideas. Too often, however, groups get lost and are unable to find their way back before running out of time. Wander off the course freely and willingly but be sure to check your bearings frequently to be sure you are still moving ahead on the topic.

Ground Rule #9

Keep it fun to keep it productive. A joke is funny because it's outside the norm. If your session is rehashing old stuff, it will have no element of newness and will probably lack revelry. Humor and flights of fancy yield double entendres, puns, and jibes. This establishes an easy atmosphere where there is no telling what your fertile mind will create. Have a good time. After all, why not?

Ground Rule #10

Embrace ambiguity. If everything in your session is clear, the session's a dud. Play in a field where the edges are blurred and there is a chance of falling into some unknown terrain. The fall is never injurious, only exhilarating.

Ground Rule #11

Foster constructive dissatisfaction. It's too easy to say something won't work or has no basis. Try expressing your concerns in terms like "I wish . . ." or "How to . . ." If someone says, "Make it big," don't say, "It won't fit." Ask, "How can we make it bigger and still have it fit?" That will spur more thinking about solutions instead of limiting thinking to the fact that it won't fit.

Ground Rule #12

Nothing "bad." Keep the word "bad" out of your session. In fact, keep it our of your vocabulary. By simply turning the word bad into the word "different" or "unique" you open up a world of new thinking. "Bad" things are repugnant. Different things can be challenging, charming, and provocative. This applies to your life and your group. A "different" world is fun. A "bad" world is just that!

Guidelines for Group Members

A creative group is six to twelve people working together to clarify a situation, solve a problem, or generate new ideas for later refinement. The energy and enthusiasm generated by a well-oiled creative group can produce great ideas and many wonderful side effects. When a creative group gets rolling, you'll notice the people in it and around it start to:

- explore new perspectives

- build stronger teams

- advocate new ideas

- support creative thinking

- think outside the limits of their day-to-day lives

- bring more fun into the process

It is common to find the residue of these side effects far beyond the realm of the creative group. This is one excellent reason to join and support creative groups whenever you can.

There is, however, an even more compelling reason to join a creative group: your personal development. In every respect, a well-run creative group is a unique environment. It is a safe haven. Within this haven you can test your creative wings with impunity—not an option in most situations.

How you participate in a creative group speaks volumes to you about you. Study your own actions and learn from them. Find out if your thinking is rigid and rule-bound or if it's open and accepting. Learn how comfortable you are with ambiguous ideas. Discover your stumbling blocks to creativity and your style of working with others in a liberated setting.

Most meetings are so structured and political it's impossible to offer up misty, vaporous ideas without being ridiculed or becoming suspect. The lively essence of a truly creative session contradicts exactly the limiting structure in most meetings. Great creative sessions demand ambiguity and reward vaporous ideas. Creative groups shamelessly open forbidden doors, stride boldly through them and journey confidently into uncharted territory. This is often a pole away from those agenda-driven meetings in the board room.

The creative journey, however, is not everyone's cup of sassafras. There are pitfalls. You will have to work as part of a team. This means that your great idea will not be yours at all. It will be the child of the *team's* creative energy. At times you will have to let go of ideas you think are earth-shattering. Sometimes you'll want everyone else to see your idea exactly the way you do. They won't. For others to see what you see, you'll have to construct it for them, with words, with actions, or at the easel with a marker in hand. If you can't tolerate people laughing at your drawings or your animated charades, sassafras may not be your cup of tea.

Or is it?

Have courage.

You'll have to learn to abandon years of relying on negative, knee-jerk responses to new ideas. You'll be asked, and will ask others, to question the hallowed boundaries and assumptions that define your environment. Not an easy charge. The reward, however, is a new set of eyes through which you will see the world in startlingly refreshing ways.

Why you?

You have been asked to join a creative group for one or more of the following reasons:

- **you have a special talent for creative thinking**

- **you will be affected by the results of the session**

- **you will be charged with putting the plan into action**

- **you are a warm body and they have an empty chair.**

Forget every reason except the first. Assume you have been asked to participate because you are the most creative person ever to warm that meeting room chair. Ignore anything, and everything, that keeps you from participating. Remember, you are on the CREATIVE TEAM. Play the part.

In addition to the "creative team," your group will consist of:

- A *facilitator* **to set up the session and keep it moving.**

- A *"client"* **to help the facilitator stay on track and to clarify information.**

- A *recorder* **to capture ideas, or the essence of an idea, and write these on large easel pads for everyone to see.**

In a well-oiled group, these roles operate smoothly. Ideas flow seamlessly one into the next. Members recognize each other's contributions and add to them without becoming protective or bogging down in who does or doesn't get credit.

It's not always so neat, however. Some groups fall into predictable traps which can dull their creative edge and limit their potential success.

Here are some traps to look out for and avoid:

A quest for order. Every creative group must follow a process. But that process should be a guide, *not an anchor.* If rigidity becomes the cornerstone, expect to birth very few new ideas.

Too little order. The delicate balance between too much and too little order is difficult to achieve. Too much order and no ideas flow. Too little order and the flow of ideas leads nowhere and the session accomplishes nothing. Keep the process on track but enjoy the side trips.

A need to belong. If group members don't express murky thoughts for fear of being ostracized, expect few fresh ideas. It takes courage to push the envelope and people with a need to belong will lick, close, and seal the envelope at all costs.

A fear of conflict. If there were no issue in question or contention, there would be no need for a creative session. Conflict, therefore, is a fact of the creative group's life. Understand it is part of the process and have no fear of expressing contrary ideas. It is the facilitator's job to keep things on an even keel, not yours. If there is conflict, let the facilitator direct it. Your job is to listen and to express your own thoughts.

Power and the need to be in control. There may be people in your creative group with a driving need to control everything. Because they believe they have the most salient ideas, they dominate the conversation, credit no other ideas, and contribute to no ideas except their own. A good facilitator can throttle this person, but it's not easy. Be on guard for this kind of person and DON'T BE ONE! If you want to profit from your participation in a group, leave your drive for power and control at home. You will be amazed at how much you can gain by simply letting go.

Assumptions. The brain is a fantastic organ. It is designed to keep life on track. Most of what it accomplishes, it does by establishing patterns and habits and sticking to them without thinking. In life, that's great. It keeps things moving. In a creative session, it's life threatening. Leave habitual, knee-jerk thinking out in the hall. Just because it has always been done that way is no reason to do it that way now. In a productive creative session, question everything. "Why is that a limit?" "What are we leaving out?" "What are we not including?" "What are we trying to avoid in this kind of thinking?" "Are we afraid the guys upstairs won't like it?" Assumptions and patterns keep life moving in an established direction. Your group's charge is to change direction. Assume nothing and you open everything.

The Session

The warm up period at the beginning of a creative session is your opportunity to set the stage for how you will act. If the facilitator asks you to think of all the things you can do with a brick, go a little crazy. "Use them as exercise shoes" might be the first thing that pops into your head. Say it! It may get a laugh and open the door for the rest of the group to be equally at ease presenting "wild" ideas. Let the craziness come out early. It will set a tone.

Once you have finished the warm-up, you will be presented with a problem. Be sure you fully understand the problem as it is given. If not, ask for clarification. Paraphrase your understanding to be sure. Chances are if it's unclear to you, it's unclear to someone else. They won't ask. You will.

The facilitator will determine the specific process the group will follow. She will explain this process to you and expect you to help keep the session on track. Remember, you are in the session to solve a problem. Keep that in mind at all times and work with a vengeance in that direction. No matter how many great ideas you have or how exciting the session, it is a dismal failure if a problem remains unsolved.

If you feel your session gets off its intended course, feel free to stop and ask the group some questions: "Why is this session off-track?" "How can we get it back on-track?" Not all groups or sessions will flow with ease. Taking a station break can steer your session back in the right direction again.

The session is done.

Your group has solved the problem. You've also made some very important personal headway. That little spark of creativity you never thought you had can burn with a startling intensity. It feels great.

You now also have a new perspective on group dynamics and the power of a "safe" environment. You have learned there are a thousand ways to look at a problem, and if you dig in your heels with a limited view, you also dig in your mind. It's a great lesson, and you will take this new learning into everything you do. After all, it was a lot more fun than those agenda-driven meetings, wasn't it? And since you were such a perfect group member, maybe it's time to try your hand at facilitating. All you need do is take a chance and turn the page.

Guidelines for Facilitators

You've decided to take the plunge and lead a group. Congratulations. It's time to take charge, to become a creative ramrod. A productive creative session is just what your business needs. Make it happen.

Facilitating, or leading a session, is *not* a group effort. When two or three people try to run a session at the same time, it becomes disjointed with little hope of maintaining cohesion and direction. If you are in charge, stay in charge. If you are working as a co-facilitator, sit down or stand aside when your partner is leading. There should be no confusion about who's in charge at any point.

Your first charge as a facilitator of a creative session is to establish and maintain an environment where people feel free to participate, an environment without hidden agendas or power plays. If you, as facilitator, sense the presence of a hidden agenda, delay the session until this impediment is cleared. If you can't correct this situation, your first session needs to focus on how to clear the environment of political obstacles.

What should you expect from your session?

There are four possible answers to this question:

1) **a complete solution to a problem**
2) **a partial solution to a problem**
3) **a re-definition of a problem**
4) **a pile of ideas in response to a problem or situation.**

Just because you don't walk out with a "Eureka!" solution or idea, doesn't mean your session failed. Sometimes gaining a better understanding of a problem is the most you can hope for and will pave the way for more progress next time.

As facilitator, you wear many hats which may include those of referee, psychologist, shadow boxer, and animal trainer. You'll sometimes need to change hats in the middle of a sentence, so it's important to keep them all handy. To do this, remain constantly focused on the goal of your session. Keep your group pointed in the right direction and hat changes will become automatic and smooth.

As facilitator you will:

- Define the session's goal.

- Establish a clear set of expectations.

- Recruit participants.

- Choose a neutral site and set it up for most effective results.

- Set the atmosphere for the session.

- Foster communications.

- Direct conflict.

- Encourage participation.

- Keep the session moving toward the goal.

- Keep your ego out of it.

Now that you know the facilitator's responsibilities, it's time to get started.

Step 1: The Problem

After discussing the situation with the person for whom you are running the session (the "client"), your first step is to construct a *clear objective* for the session. This Problem Statement or Session Objective should be designed to achieve two goals:

1) satisfy the needs of the "client"
2) encourage participation by the group

Be sure you know exactly what your "client" would like to have at session's end. Don't settle for vague direction such as "just a bunch of ideas." Your group will be unsure of its direction, you will wind up with nothing of use, and your "client" won't be happy. Create a Problem Statement/Session Objective which establishes clear direction as in these examples (see Introduction to Problems/Opportunities in Part 3 for more information on this):

"Identify four ways to improve weekly reporting of sales contacts."

"Identify three ways to improve communications between data processing and marketing."

"Define actions to establish a more creative environment within the company."

Make sure your group understands that the numbers refer to resulting ideas, not the number of ideas generated along the way. Keep track of all ideas generated. Many times an overlooked idea becomes a centerpiece once the dust settles.

Once you have your Problem Statement/Session Objective, write it on a large sheet of paper and keep it ready for the session. Remember, everything revolves around this.

After you formulate your statement and before the session begins, you should create a guide or outline for the session. Go over this with the "client" to be sure your session will cover all relevant issues. Do this enough in advance of the session to allow for modifications. The Briefing Document, discussed in Part 3, is a useful tool in this process.

Step 2: The Process

Decide on the actual problem-solving process you will use in the session. Classic Brainstorming is a great technique for the first-time facilitator. It is a fine place to start because it requires no formal training, is easy to set up, and has flexibility. This and other techniques are explained in detail in Part 3.

No matter which technique you choose, it is critical that everyone in the group follow certain basic rules which enhance the "safety" and, therefore, the productivity of your session. You must make these rules clear and hold people to them. In his book, *Applied Imagination*, Alex Osborne lists four primary rules for keeping creative sessions open:*

1) *Avoid criticism.* It's the biggest idea killer around.

2) *Free-wheel.* Presenting your wildest ideas is expected and encouraged.

3) *Shoot for quantity.* You can always throw out what you don't want later.

4) *Combine and improve.* Often called hitchhiking, group members should add to or modify others' ideas.

The Hurt Rule: No waves, no ripple, no wake . . . you were never there.

At the end of the allotted time, you will choose either to close the session with a long list of ideas or to find the few ideas with the most potential. There are a couple of criteria that can help guide your group in determining which ideas may prove most successful. Ask your group:

- **Which ideas contain an element of newness or novelty? This should be assessed from the "client's" point of view, not yours.**

*These rules overlap the *"Ground Rules"* and *"Guidelines for Participants"* mentioned earlier. You should review them carefully prior to your session and ask your group members to review also.

- Which ideas are at least somewhat feasible? Which will the "client" consider working with? Notice the words "somewhat" and "consider." Don't forget the whole reason for a creative session is to generate new ideas which often live on the fringe. Don't get skittish now.

Step 3: The Group

There are four categories of group participants:

- the facilitator

- the recorder

- the "client"

- the group members (the creative engine).

The Facilitator

As facilitator, you must understand the roles, rights, and responsibilities of the other participants so you can assist each of them in fulfilling his or her purpose.

The Recorder

When your group gets hot, ideas and vague notions will come out at an incredible clip. Your job as facilitator is to listen carefully, keep the process in order, and explore the vague notions. It is better, therefore, not to be writing but to have someone else keeping notes on the large newsprint pads. This is the job of the recorder.

He or she writes each thought down in full view of the group. When your group is on a roll, this can be a taxing job. A good recorder abbreviates and uses shorthand to grab each idea as it spins out into the ether. The best ideas are often bolts of inspiration and must be captured at that moment or lost forever. Distill long thoughts to a few key words. Space and time are limited. Tell the participants if they have an idea while someone else is talking, write it down. Don't let it get away. They'll have their turn.

A critical aspect of the recorder's job is not to alter the ideas in the process of getting them down on paper. The recorder and you, the facilitator, must check carefully to be sure each idea is recorded accurately. Paraphrasing is an excellent technique to employ here. Repeat the participant's idea back to her in your own words. If she approves, write it down. If not, continue going back and forth until you get approval, then write it down.

If there is any doubt or ambiguity about an idea, stop everything until it is cleared up and accurately written down. Often this act of clarifying stimulates new ideas. Be sure you capture those as well.

Have your recorder number each page and each idea as it is presented. This lets you to refer to ideas by number if necessary.

The "Client"

There are times when having someone in the group to serve as a "client" can be very beneficial. This person does not have to be your actual "client" but someone you can turn to if you need a bit of hard information, a new insight into the problem, or a clarification on details. Remember, you are not and should not be the expert. You do your job of facilitating better when you can be most objective. It helps, therefore, to have someone in the group you can turn to if the situation demands expert knowledge.

There are some people *not* to have as a "client" in your group:

- **A person who may be the cause of the problem.**

- **A person who acts like "the boss."**

- **A person who thinks he already "knows" the answer.**

- **A person who has a hidden agenda, whose presence you feel will inhibit the group.**

If any of these people end up in your group, it is your responsibility to keep control of them and not let them hinder your progress. Choose your "expert" or "client" with care.

The Group Members

As a rule, a productive group consists of *between five and twelve people*. With less, the group becomes a chat session; with more, control slips. Determining the make-up of your group is one of your responsibilities and will be a major determinant in the success of your session. The very best group, however, has no chance of success if you, as facilitator, do not do your job. There are no bad audiences, only bad actors.

Stock your session with the right people. Some factors to consider:

- **You may want to include *one or two people who will be affected by the outcome of the session*. If they are involved at the inception, they will be more likely to help with the implementation. However, don't overload your session with these people. They can't help but bring some prejudices that could slow the process. "Tried that," "Done that," "Seen that," have no place in any session. Choose these folks with special care.**

- Include *one or two people with some technical knowledge about the problem.* They will add necessary input about the topic. Again, don't overload your group with these people. Their depth of knowledge may add confusion and can make the less informed feel ill at ease.

- The rest of your group should be comprised of a *variety of personalities.* There are no rules, only guidelines. First, look for people who interact well with individuals as well as groups. This kind of person sits up, looks you in the eye, and has a facility for getting others to talk. This may well be the guy that delivers the sandwiches at lunch or the gal who works down the hall. Obviously, if you are screening for people with specific experience, you can't choose just anybody. If, however, you know people who you believe have traits which will benefit your session, recruit them.

If you plan to conduct many sessions, keep a file. Have people fill out a form that will help you screen for exactly what you may need. In addition to name, rank, and serial number, find out about hobbies, past employment, and education. You never know what you may need.

In some cases you will have to pay your participants a fee. Depending on where you are and the level of expertise you require, this can be from a few dollars to a couple of hundred. Often a lunch or dinner will be all that is needed for internal people. Don't be cheap. If you need a specific type of participant, spend the money. This investment can pay off in multiples.

Another guideline, recruit people willing to present thoughts or ideas without getting married to them. They should also be willing to give credit, take credit, build on other's ideas, stick to the topic, and not be afraid to play in the lush field of fantasy.

Always remember that this is your group and you are in charge. Your group will achieve the goal by your direction, so choose carefully.

Step 4: The Location

Always hold your session in a neutral setting, not in someone's office. You don't want participants feeling like they are in someone else's domain and you don't want the occupant to feel intruded upon or territorial. Find a large room with lots of space to spread out. If you need to break down into smaller groups, you will need space.

If your facility doesn't have a large enough room, hold your session in a hotel conference room where you can be provided with the items you will need such as easels, markers, pads, and audio-visual equipment. A few hours away from "the office" can be very liberating, adding just that much more spark to your session.

Step 5: The Set-up

Set up the room in a "U" formation with you, the recorder, and the easel pads at the open end. This way people can see each other as well as the notes. If you intend to break into smaller groups, you may be better served if the room is set with round tables to accommodate five or six people each. Be sure to have an easel pad for each group and separate the tables as much as possible to lessen confusion.

There should be ample wall space to tape up filled newsprint sheets. Be sure to have plenty of masking tape, markers, newsprint pads, water, and a legal pad and pencil for each participant. Room temperature is important also. Don't let the room get too hot; cool is better.

Step 6: The Housekeeping

Set each participant's place before they arrive with paper, water, any handouts, and a 5" X 8" index card. Have them fold the index card lengthwise and write their first name on it in big letters. You will need to see everyone's name. Tell them about parking validation, breaks, bathroom locations, and the time you will be completed. If you invite the members by memo, cover these points in the memo and review them again at the beginning of the session. If you told them you will be finished at a specific time, finish at that time—that's a rule! There is life outside your session.

Step 7: The Start

Everybody's in place and you're on! Kicking off the session is instrumental in establishing the tone for what follows. A simple "thank you for coming" is a dandy way to get things rolling. This is the time to let people know how you feel about the process and what you are expecting. Here are some points that may help.

Let them know

- You have no vested interest in the outcome. Your job is to keep things going, not to express opinions.

- There are no right or wrong answers or ideas.

- Every idea has merit in itself or as a lead into something else.

- They should leave criticism outside.

- If something is not clear, you will ask for clarification or you will try to paraphrase it. They should also ask if a point is confusing.

- They have the brains and ideas, your job is to drain out everything you can.

- You want a lot of ideas.

- Everyone should feel free to add to (or hitchhike on) someone else's ideas.

It's time to get everyone talking. Your objective at this stage is to loosen up the group and gain some insight into the individual members. Here are some topics to use as a guide (it's great if you remember the information and can use it later in the session):

- Name?

- Where they live?

- Family pets . . . dog, cat, exotic fish?

- Hobbies?

- Current work position?

- Ever been in a session before?

- Expectation of this session?

You may find one answer offers a new line of questions; yield to it and see where it takes you. There are no hard and fast rules here. Just remember to keep it conversational. If you are formal and uptight, your group will respond in kind. It is easy to have someone get long-winded here so be sure not to dwell on these introductions. Also, don't miss anyone. This is your chance and theirs to get a feel for the environment. Let it flow, keep it light.

Step 8: The Warm-up

A warm-up exercise should be used to get everyone talking. A broad question like, "What do you consider the primary characteristics of a creative person and why?" can serve as an interesting springboard. Another option is to ask for alternate uses of a common object. "As fast as you can, think of other uses for a clothespin." Give the group a minute or two, then open the floor.

It is best at first to address one person in the group. "OK, Joe, give us some of your thoughts." Move around the room or call on anyone anxious to contribute. Have your recorder write down the ideas so everyone gets a feel for the process. This is a great chance for you to use humor and make the exercise fun. If someone suggests something unusual for clothespins like, "hold the sheets down," don't just move on. Pause and let everyone imagine what that person may mean. You can simply say, "Sheets?" The rest of the group will understand the humor, and then you can move on.

This exercise should last 10 to 15 minutes. Once everyone has contributed an idea or two, close the warm-up and move to the next stage.

Step 9: The Attack

Tape your Problem Statement/Session Objective up on the wall so everyone can see it. If you sent out the statement in the initial communication, the group will have had a few days to think about it. Your objective now is to be sure the statement is clear and everyone is in agreement with it as stated. Take a few minutes before you begin your main activity to explore other points of view. If the participants agree that the statement needs some modification and, if the modifications don't change the fundamental nature of the statement, revise it. This will instill a strong sense of ownership in the group and encourage more participation.

Before you ask your group to generate ideas, you may want to prime the creative pump with a bit of information. Review the Briefing Document in Part 3 and either you or the "client" can bring everyone up to speed.

While the points from the Briefing Document are being discussed, have your group members make notes on ideas or notions that pop into their heads. The mind is an amazing organ. If we give it some room, it will perform feats of magic. It is up to you to set the tone and let it happen.

Step 10: The Session . . . Stage Center

You're off. Now you want ideas and you want lots of them. Your group is primed and armed with just enough information to get them rolling, so let's do it.

Begin the session by asking for thoughts. Again, it is best to call on one person to get things going. This is not intended to put that person on the spot and probably won't, but if you detect discomfort, tell him he can pass and move on to someone else. Once some ideas have been put forth, you can go back and ask how others feel about them. This provides a less threatening opportunity to get involved.

Here are some methods that will help you gain the most from the group:

- **Ask open-ended questions using terms like: "How?" "What?" "In what ways?" As a rule, if the question can be answered with a simple yes or no, you will not generate much information or new thinking.**

- **Ask for examples.**

- Ask other members if they feel the same way about a point. Why? Why not?

- Look for similarities between points.

- Look for differences between points.

- If someone starts to make a point and backs off because it is too much like a point already made, have her tell you anyway. You never know.

- If conflict occurs (and hope it does), have the conflicting parties argue the other's point of view.

- Bring everyone out. If you find some members will not participate at all, you may be forced to leave them alone for a while. Try to lure them in by asking for simple feedback on others' ideas. Keep trying. Be gentle and encouraging. Be aware that some people just take longer.

- If in doubt, paraphrase. Ask others to paraphrase.

- If an idea is way out in left field, see if the group can bring it into focus. Call on different people in the group to gain a new perspective.

- Remain neutral and don't compete. Even if you love the sound of your own voice, or if you flip over an idea, keep a lid on it; it's not your session. Let the group be definitive, not you. The position you command up in front of the room is very powerful. It is easy to manipulate the group toward one position. Guard against that at all costs.

- Don't let one person dominate. If you find that happening you can:

  ▲ Direct questions away from that person.

  ▲ Ask that person to "hold that thought for a second."

  ▲ Tell him/her that you need another point of view.

  ▲ Ask him/her to "make a note of it and you'll get back to it."

If this person does not slow down, it may be necessary to take him aside at a break and ask him to assume a lower posture. Not that you don't want the input. Its just that you feel others are holding back. Never attack a group member. Everyone else will wonder if they will be next and your group will shut down.

- The three most powerful words in the facilitator's book of tricks: *Tell me more*. These words work magic in encouraging people to give their best. All ideas are fragile at birth. These three words allow room for growth and exploration.

- Always listen with your third ear. That's the ear that hears what is not being said, the non-verbal and the intonation. If your group is active and leaning forward, you are working on an idea that may have merit. If the guy in the back rolls his eyes and folds his arms, let him know you saw it and ask him what he's thinking. Be sure you do this in a non-accusatory manner. He may just be folding his arms. Look for general agreement or disagreement. You will know you have it when the group is nodding and attentive. Find out why they all agree or disagree. Let people know you hear them, see them, and want to capture what they have to say. It will make everyone want to contribute.

If your group starts to run out of gas, use The Game (Part 5) or another technique to get things going again. Planning ahead for this eventuality and having a trick or two up your sleeve can be a real session saver.

In every group there will be conflict. It is a necessary and potent ingredient in creativity. To gain the most from a conflict:

- Clarify each point. Restate or paraphrase.

- Look for similarities in points of view.

- Have other members of the group re-state the conflicting points.

- Ask other members of the group about the conflict.

- Have the conflicting parties argue the other's point.

One technique for resolving a conflict or determining the worth of an idea is to conduct a BenBalance. Review the BenBalance procedure (presented in Part 6) before your session and be ready to make the most of conflict.

Step 11: The Close

You have just spent the past few hours facilitating a group. It is time to bring it to a close. If your problem statement required you to "Come up with five ideas that will expedite the reporting of sales leads," then you will need to go back over the list of ideas and find the five most promising ones. Given the vast number of ideas generated, this may appear to be an insurmountable task. It's not. Here are a few steps that will help:

1) Give the group five or ten minutes to review all the notes taped up on the wall.

2) Have everyone write down the ten ideas they think come the closest to answering the problem.

3) Have them rank their selections. To do this, give everyone 100 points. They must weigh

each idea by giving it some of those points. If a participant thinks idea 49 is just great, he may want to assign it 60 points. That will leave him 40 points to divide between his remaining 9 selections.

4) Once everyone has tallied up their selections, go around the room and have everyone report their selections and the number of points assigned and note the totals next to the idea.

5) Add up the totals for each idea and rank the top five.

Life is not perfect. You may not end up with a clear top five. In this case, have everyone review only the items that have received any points at all and then have them re-choose and assign points to these choices. You may get some grumbling about having to choose from a list that was not a first choice. Press on. Your job is to answer the needs of the "client," and this is the best way to do it.

Once you have your list of the top five, if time permits, you can conduct a BenBalance (Part 6) on each idea. This can be done quickly with limited discussion. It is a great way to gather a few more gems or test for holes that will need patching.

Ask if there are any final thoughts, feelings or suggestions, thank everyone, tell them they did a great job, give them their reward, and send them home.

Step 12: The End

You're beat. A hard-driving session takes it out of you, but it's a great feeling. Take down the sheets and put them in order. Have someone type them right away, before they get cold. Take the top five ideas along with the BenBalance information and type that separately. This is the hard-core information you were after. Don't let anything happen to the other sheets. You or your "client" will want to go over those ideas just in case something jumps out.

Make a few notes on the participants. If they were good, you may want to use them again.

Congratulations!! You have just facilitated your first session. No doubt there were a few slips. Maybe a fall or two. So what! It will be easier next time and easier the time after that. If you like facilitating, find a book or two and learn some new techniques, but don't expect to become a facilitator by knowing techniques. You learn facilitating by facilitating. The more you do it, the better you do it. Stick with it.

After all is said and done, there is an even greater benefit. You will become better at getting the best from the people around you. You'll learn that most of the time we have no idea what other people really think. You'll learn that generally we talk out of inspiration and vague hope that the random thoughts, ideas, notions, and speculations that enter our heads will find an opportunity to be listened to and explored.

Now that you are a big-shot facilitator, you have the skills to help that happen for the people around you. Be ready. A vista of creativity is about to open up before you. It will open doors others see as having no handle and take you places you may not even have dreamed of. Prepare yourself, open your mind, and most of all be ready to have fun.

PART 3

Finding, Presenting, and Clarifying Opportunities

(Often Disguised as Problems)

Problem/Opportunity Introduction

One of the primary hallmarks of a creative person or organization is the ability to find opportunities that may be invisible to others. This may seem like a mystical power, but in reality it results from nothing more than attentive, persistent hard work.

This section explains several techniques you can use to find opportunities (often disguised as problems), clarify the essential issues within these problems/opportunities, and create Problem Statements/Session Objectives that will put your sessions on the right track.

The importance of finding problems/opportunities and then presenting them in clear and directed Problem Statements/Session Objectives can not be overstated. How many times has a small problem, unseen and unaddressed, grown into a major crisis taking massive amounts of energy, effort, and valuable time to get under control? Imagine how easy it would have been to avoid the whole fiasco if you had discovered the problem early enough. Similarly, how many times have you knocked yourself out to solve a problem and produced an effective plan only to realize that you have fixed the "wrong" problem? Imagine the savings in time and effort if you had been working on the "right" problem from the beginning.

The techniques presented in this section will help you to find problems before they get out of hand and to discover opportunities you might never have seen before. They will also help you identify the key aspects of *problems/opportunities* so you can focus your work on their most productive elements. Combining both of these processes will pay handsome dividends by saving time and energy, and improving morale. Using these techniques well will also make your creative efforts look almost magical. Who couldn't use a pat on the back from the people upstairs?

Two terms you have seen previously and will see a lot of in the following pages deserve a bit more explanation here. These are Problem Statement and Session Objective. A Problem Statement/Session Objective is a one- to two- sentence statement which does two things:

1) It clearly identifies the problem/opportunity, focusing attention on its key aspects.

2) It invites participation and sets direction and goals for the session.

Here are some examples of effective Problem Statements/Session Objectives (for more examples, see Guidelines for Facilitators in Part 2):

- List 25 ideas for handling incoming mail more efficiently.

- Identify four ways to reduce order backlogs.

- Provide six alternatives to staff meetings to increase communication between departments.

• **Define actions to establish a more effective employee review process.**

As you can see, the wording of the Problem Statement/Session Objective can have a significant impact on the kind of session you will run. You can ask for a large number of ideas, leaving evaluation of the ideas for another time. Or, you can work towards narrowing down the number of ideas during the session to the few which have the best chance of solving the problem.

Whatever choices you make, be sure to use these techniques to help you create statements/objectives which get you on the road toward effective solutions to the "right" problems.

Opportunity Exploratory Sessions (OESs)

Problems are opportunities in disguise and, as you may have noticed, problems are everywhere. Sometimes, they're right in front of you. Other times you have to look for them. For an organization to prosper, it can't wait for problems to come to it; it has to go out looking for them. If everyone is on the prowl for potential problems, then a simple situation won't become a full-blown calamity and demand more time, effort, and money to resolve than if intercepted early.

Opportunities have a stealth quality. They often start out as small almost unseen ideas, observations, or notions and can quickly grow into big bucks. Unlike problems, they don't creep up on you uninvited. Indeed, they are often lying right in front of you, but, before you recognize them, they are grabbed by someone else and you are left holding the empty bag.

To intercept problems before they explode or to search out opportunities before they slip away, you should conduct regular Opportunity Exploratory Sessions (OESs). An OES is simply a group of people from within the company looking around, exploring their environment, asking questions, discussing the answers, and speculating on how to turn ideas and observations into new opportunities.

Setting up an OES is simple, but there are some preliminary steps to take to assure success.

First: *Talk to management about the idea of an OES.* If management doesn't at least buy into the concept, spend your time elsewhere; the project will have no longevity. Let management know your objective is to start a program that will encourage everyone to take a close look at their work and their environment in order to find opportunities to make them better, more effective, efficient, fertile, and profitable. Let management know this group will be charged with asking a simple question like, "Do we have an opportunity?" These opportunities can be in any phase of the operation: improving distribution; streamlining customer service; creating a day-care center for employee children; or finding a better way to get rid of the trash. The answers will be reviewed by the members of the OES group to determine if they offer any possibilities. If they do, these ideas will be fleshed out and presented to management.

Second: *Appoint an Opportunity Ramrod* . . . you could choose yourself—after all, you're taking the initiative to read this book! The Ramrod's responsibility is to get things rolling. She sets up the meetings, collects ideas, facilitates discussions, and follows up with management. The Ramrod needs to be a person with drive and perseverance; someone who doesn't mind challenging established orders. In short, a Ramrod is a "renegade" with the ability to make things happen. Every growing company has a covey of these people. They are often the ones who complain their creativity is stifled and they feel restricted. Unrestrict them by making them the Ramrod(s) of an OES. The Ramrod's job can be tough, but it can also be more fun and rewarding than any other position in the company.

Third: *The Ramrod will need to select a group.* There is no single profile that best describes a member of an OES group, so start by finding people who are intrinsically motivated. Find people who need little direction and who accept the challenges and risks of an OES group with open arms. Other favorable characteristics are a keen eye for details, a willingness to ask questions about everything, and a capacity to talk about ideas without bias. These people may be difficult to find at first. Once your group gets going, they'll find you.

Even though the people you want in your group are intrinsically motivated, including their participation in the OES group as part of their performance review will add some high-test extrinsic motivation . . . a powerful combination. You may be able to offer some kind of reward to anyone offering an idea that saves or earns the company money. This can be a percentage of the savings or a bonus. Talk to management about this as an inducement to the OES group members or to anyone proposing an idea that saves or produces money.

Fourth: *Hold your first meeting.* This meeting is by far the most important one you will have. It is here that you will set the tone for the group and the program. Ideally, the president of the company will attend. She will champion the effort and let everyone know they have her full support. Ideal, but don't depend on it. Most of the time you will find lip service is the best you can expect. Don't let that deter you; press on. If the president "can't make it," the job will fall to the Ramrod. The Ramrod must find the right words to motivate the group and have it believe in the project.

Some points to be included in your first meeting:

- **Explain that every member of the group has been hand-selected because they have the talents required to make an OES sing. They are the risk takers and challengers—the people who are always trying to improve things.**

- **Their charge is to look at and question everything within the organization, from trash to elevators, parking to marketing. Nothing should escape their eyes or their exploration. Make sure they understand that they are not on a "mission," and that they have no authority or duty to**

back someone into a corner. All you want them to do is keep an eye open for opportunities and ask leading questions.

- Let everyone know that any information they are given is confidential and will remain confidential. You want the unvarnished truth, and if a source of sensitive information is exposed, the group may as well disband because you'll get no more.

- The mind-set is simple: *constructive dissatisfaction*, no negativity. This means look at problems as opportunities with an eye towards solutions—not just restatements of the problem.

- If something seems out of whack, the person finding the "out of whack" situation should use the Opportunity Exploratory Note Pad (simply a pad of paper left in a private area accessible to all OES group members) to write down what they think needs attention. These notes will become the fodder for the next OES meeting.

Fifth: *Arrange to have various departments in the company make presentations to the OES group.* These shouldn't just be presentations of problems. Instead, have them tell you what their department does and how it goes about doing it. Ask them about the kind of opportunities they have had and how have they addressed them. What kind of equipment does their department have and what other jobs can it perform? Ask them to explain what the competition does. What is the competition doing differently from us? How do their ads look? How do ours look and why are we saying what we are in the copy? Fill the OES members' minds with a broad range of facts from throughout the company so the OES's talents and capabilities can be instrumental in solving problems or generating opportunities throughout your company.

Sixth: *At each meeting, discuss the ideas or opportunities presented by group members to determine if they have potential.* If the group thinks an idea has merit, write it up and present it to management. At that point the job of the OES group is done. If management wants your group to move to the next stage of problem solution or opportunity exploration, other sections of this book tell you how to proceed. Don't be surprised if your next group session is a creative session.

Seventh: *Set up a schedule for your follow-up meetings.* It is best if you set a schedule for at least the next three meetings. Calendars tend to get full and you want to make sure your OES group members are available.

Keep good records of all the thoughts, questions, and ideas your group comes up with and review them from time to time. Conditions and circumstances change and an idea or errant notion that falters today may blossom in a month.

Opportunity Exploratory Session Worksheet

OPPORTUNITY

_____

_____

How did you get the idea? _____

Where were you? _____

Who was with you? _____

Were they part of the idea? _____

How? _____

Will they help you/us refine the idea? _____

What prompted the idea? _____

_____

_____

What are your initial thoughts on how to bring this notion into sharper focus? _____

_____

_____

What do you like about this notion? _____

Concerns? _____

_____

What/who do you need to take this opportunity to the next stage? _____

_____

_____

_____

PROJECT NAME _____   DATE _____ PG. _____ OF _____

Brain Chain Reaction

Just as there is more than one way to get where you are going—there is more than one way to identify potential opportunities, often disguised as problems. Conducting Opportunity Exploratory Sessions (see preceeding section) is not the only way. The following technique can be just as effective.

Brain Chain Reaction

Get together six people you believe to have good insight into the day-to-day operation of your organization. In the meeting have each of them list three problems they think exist within your organization. You now have a total of 18 potential opportunities.

Next, have each person show his list to another member of the group. The two of them work together to narrow their six problems down to three. Next, have each pair arrange their three problems in descending order of importance. You now have a total of nine problem statements (three sets of three). The most important problem/opportunity should be at the top of each list. If you want, you can either discuss each problem/opportunity or collect all the lists and analyze them yourself. This technique will provide you with a great place to start if you are charged with searching out problems/opportunities.

Problem/Opportunity Clarification

Identifying one or many problems is an important first step toward grasping opportunities. Now it is time to capitalize. But before you go out to conquer the beast, you had better be damn sure you are not attacking the next door neighbor's prized pet, or building a campfire in the middle of a natural gas refinery. *Clarifying your problem/opportunity is well worth the time, energy, and effort.* It is much better than generating and implementing a foolproof plan only to find out you fixed the wrong problem or the wrong aspect of the problem.

There are several techniques you can choose from to help you clarify and focus your Problem Statement/Session Objective. Formulating a clear, directed, results-oriented Problem Statement/Session Objective can take you miles toward the correct solution. Which method you choose is less important than investing yourself and your group in this part of the process.

The three techniques which follow will help you determine the true essence of your problem/opportunity and how to phrase it as a Problem Statement or Session Objective which will engage your group and give it the direction it needs to solve the problem. The next section, Briefing Document, provides more information both on identifying the correct problem and refining its presentation for maximum results.

What then, What then, What then

Once you think you have identified a problem/opportunity, ask a trilogy of "*what then*" questions to be sure you are at the heart of it.

For example, assume there is a major thunderstorm going on outside and you are trying to finish reading a report for a meeting in an hour. Every few minutes the lights flicker out and then flicker back on. What's your problem here? Chances are your first answer is, "an electrical problem caused by the storm." To get you to the heart of the problem ask the "*what then*" questions:

- **The first "*what then*" question, "When there is an electrical storm, what then?" tells you "During an electrical storm the lights can go out."**

- **The second "*what then*" question, "If the lights go out, what then?" yields "It's dark."**

- **The third "*what then*" question, "When it's dark, what then?" leads to "You can't see to get your work done."**

Now you know the real problem and your course of action. You need to find a way to light the report so you can finish reading within the allotted time. If you start calling the power company or checking for fallen trees, you won't solve the problem of getting the report read. Your course of action is clear—get a flashlight, light a candle or build a fire. The critical element is to be sure you are solving the correct problem. This technique will keep you on track.

You can always call the power company later.

Attack and Defend

Once a Problem Statement/Session Objective has been presented, one or two members of the group must stand up and defend the problem as stated. The rest of the group is charged with attacking (in a productive way) the problem/opportunity as it is stated to be sure it is as clear and concise as it can be. If a change is presented and accepted, the person or persons presenting the change must now defend the new statement/objective. At the end of the attack and defend session, you should have a statement/objective that is clear and acceptable to everyone. A distinct advantage of this technique is that it helps kick-start the group into the problem-solving mode.

Redefine and Review

Once a Problem Statement/Session Objective has been presented to a group in a creative session, have everybody write down at least two different ways of presenting it. Each person reports these new statements/objectives to the group to see if they prompt new thinking or changes. It is not critical that the statement/objective be redefined, just that you are sure you have the problem well in hand.

Briefing Document

A Briefing Document has two potential uses. It can:

1) **clarify a problem before a creative session**
2) **kick-start the session itself.**

To use the Briefing Document to clarify a problem before a session, meet with the client** and use the questions on the worksheet to get a handle both on the issues to be addressed in the session and its desired outcome. Be sure to cover all the points in the Briefing Document with the client so you get a full-bodied sense of the purpose of the session and where it should go. You can use this information to generate or fine tune the Problem Statement/Session Objective, plan for the session, or introduce the statement/objective to the group at the start of the session.

To use the Briefing Document to kick off a creative session follow these steps:

1) **Have the initial (it is likely to be modified later) Problem Statement/Session Objective written on a large easel pad and placed where everyone can see it. Make sure it calls for action by using words like: "Plan a new system for . . .", "Develop five ways to . . .", or "Generate additional ways to . . .".**

2) **Present the statement/objective to the group, providing any additional general information you feel the group must have. Don't provide too much. If this information serves to clarify thinking, include it. If it seems even a little biased, you may want to leave it out. Be careful not to overinform. Too much information can serve to fix some points and some minds before the session ever begins.**

**Your client is the person who commissions the session. If there is no actual "client," it may be helpful to prepare the Briefing Document with someone who has knowledge of the problem and who might benefit from its resolution (two heads are truly better than one in preparing for your session). It is best not to use a participant from the session itself. Participants should have an uncluttered view of the problem/opportunity to keep them as open as possible during the session.

3) Work efficiently through the following questions. To save on time and multiply the ideas, have the group break into pairs or trios and answer the questions together in a sentence or two. To streamline the process, provide the questions on a handout with space for responses (see worksheet at the end of this section):

❑ What is the current situation?

❑ Why is this a problem?

❑ How did it become a problem?

❑ Who/what does the problem affect?

❑ What has been done already to solve the problem?

❑ What would be the very best possible outcome?

❑ How will we know when the problem has been solved?

❑ Are there any similar problems we have faced? What are they and what were some of the solutions?

4) Emphasizing brevity, have each pair or trio give one response to a question then move on to the next group until all new ideas on that question are exhausted. Have a recorder write the ideas on a large pad in the front of the room.

5) When all the ideas are out, ask for suggestions to improve the Problem Statement/Session Objective. Allowing the group to shape the statement/objective will enhance their invest-ment in the process and their commitment to finding a solution. Make sure any changes do not alter the basic nature of the problem/opportunity, only the way it is presented.

6) Before letting the session kick into high gear, double check that you have covered any "givens" that may be required. These should be only those items that are absolutely exempt from change, attack, modification. Keep this list short, otherwise there is really no room to be creative.

Some additional suggestions to make your work more effective:

1) When discussing the problem/opportunity, use descriptive, visual words that provoke images and thinking. Example: We all know that the copy room is no bigger than a phone booth and feels like an overcrowded subway car most of the day.

2) Present information about the problem/opportunity in a way that will invite participation. Example: "Working together, and without any restrictions, think of five ways to help hand-icapped people put out a 25-pound trash bag. Tap into everything and anything you can imagine. And don't worry about practicality. Be as wild as you can be."

3) Have group members write down every idea that pops into their heads, no matter when it comes—even in the middle of talking. No idea should be allowed to slip away. Even snip-pets of an idea need to be written down. "The shortest pencil is better than the longest memory."

4) Have them speculate with words like " I wish" and "How to." For example: "I wish we had $5 million for this project" or "How to get more people involved" may mean little at the time, but they may spur something later in the session.

The whole point to briefing the group is getting the problem out on the table, clarifying it, and getting the group thinking about solutions. Once the briefing is complete, address any concerns from the group—then plan your assault. Now that everyone has been briefed, the problem doesn't stand a chance!

Briefing Document Worksheet

PROBLEM STATEMENT/SESSION OBJECTIVE

1. *What is the current situation?* _____

   _____

2. *Why is this a problem?* _____

   _____

3. *How did it become a problem?* _____

   _____

4. *Who/what does the problem affect?* _____

   _____

5. *What has been done already to solve the problem?* _____

   _____

6. *What would be the very best possible outcome?* _____

   _____

7. *How will we know when the problem has been solved?* _____

   _____

8. *Are there any similar problems we have faced?* _____

   _____

9. *What are they and what were some of the solutions?* _____

   _____

   _____

   _____

   _____

   _____

PROJECT NAME _____   DATE _____ PG. _____ OF _____

© FLOYD HURT 1999 1 (800) THINK NU

PART 4

Nuts and Bolts:

Creative Techniques

Techniques — Introduction

The groundwork has been laid. You understand the demands of making a creative life. You realize creativity requires a certain mind-set and hard, disciplined work. You know how a creative group or session runs. You have defined a problem and checked it for accuracy. What next?

It's time to choose a creative technique with which to attack your problem or exploit your opportunity. There are several techniques presented in this chapter. Each includes an overview of a technique's strengths, such as breaking problems down, generating a volume of ideas, or establishing and assigning action steps.

Familiarize yourself with the strengths of each technique and choose carefully. Nothing kills creative momentum more quickly than a session which seems to wander or does not clearly and directly address an issue. Remember, perception is everything. Make it easy for your group members, managers, CEOs to see the benefits of the creative approach and not perceive that the session as just a get-together yielding little or nothing of value.

Of course, absolute rigidity to a technique is not the goal either. Let solutions develop, always keeping the ultimate goal in your mind and in your sights. Be willing and able to marry, mix, and match techniques. There are not, and should not be, any impermeable barriers between the techniques. Know your problem and your goals, and choose whatever technique or combination of techniques that will set you on the path toward a solution.

Note: Each of the following techniques is broken into workable steps to help first-time or inexperienced facilitators work through them. There are, however, certain assumptions about the structure of a creative session, (presented in Guidelines to Facilitators, Part 2), which are not repeated for each technique. To maximize your effectiveness and the effectiveness of your group, be sure you understand the basic structure of a creative group and a creative session. Always have a plan going into a session and at least one potential back-up plan in case things do not ignite the way you had hoped they would.

These techniques are potent. They can launch you and your group on dazzling creative journeys. But this does not all happen magically. It is the result of hard work, good planning, and a healthy dose of risk taking. Do your homework, take some risks, and the rewards will be great.

Brainstorming

The word "brainstorming" has become an almost generic term for all creative problem solving even though it is only one of hundreds of techniques that can be used. Brainstorming is not appropriate for every problem-solving situation. There are pros and cons.

Pros:

A Brainstorming Session

- Quickly generates many ideas.

- Brings in peripheral factors and ideas that can add to understanding the problem and the solution.

- Is a great way to tap into ideas and views from a variety of perspectives.

- Is a great way to build a team by putting people "through" something together.

- Often has long-term effects because initial ideas often lead to others once the session is over.

Cons:

A Brainstorming Session

- Only produces ideas, not an action plan.

- Produces ideas which sometimes are not directly related to the problem, (making it appear like a waste of time to some).

- Is not a "formal" technique. Unless you are careful, this can lead the group in circles.

- Can intimidate quieter personalities and allow some people to monopolize and dominate the session.

- Requires an open-ended problem—one that allows for speculation and different points of view.

In short, if you're looking for lots of ideas to sift through to find the jewels, Brainstorming is perfect. If you need a more formal action plan or have a problem that requires a single "right" answer, you should consider another method.

The basic rules for all creative sessions have been listed and discussed in Guidelines for Facilitators (Part 2). Because Brainstorming can be such a high-energy, often-used, idea-producing tool, the basic rules are presented again here with additional explanation. It is best to post these rules clearly on the wall at any creative session:

1) *Avoid criticism.* Every idea is welcome. Hold all negative reactions. *Every* idea is welcome. Hold *all* negative reactions. (*Need I repeat it again?*)

2) *Free-wheel.* Free-wheeling means the wilder, the better. It is always easier to tame down a wild idea than to bring a new one up! Let your mind go, and go, and then go again. No holds barred.

3) *Shoot for quantity.* The more ideas you have, the more you have to choose from and the more likely you are to spark even more ideas. Always go for one or two more ideas.

4) *Combine and improve.* Ideas spark ideas. If someone says something that generates a new idea in you, write it down or bring it up. Don't assume your idea is like anyone else's . . . it isn't, it never can be.

The Hurt Rule: No waves, no ripples, no wake . . . you were never there.

All the other general rules and guidelines covered earlier apply to any Brainstorming Session.

The basic steps in a Brainstorming Session:

Step 1: Warming Up

Just as in athletics, singing, acting, or any other activity which pushes you to your limits, a good warm-up can make a huge difference in your results. Provide your session participants with some quick activity which will get them ready to leap outside their normal boundaries. You can find more specific advice on this in Guidelines for Facilitators (Part 2).

Step 2: Appoint a Recorder

This person will record the ideas in the front of the room on large newsprint sheets (This is the best method so you can walk out of the room with the originals for future reference, rather than copying it all off of a chalk or dry erase board.) The only requirements here are willingness and reasonably neat and fast handwriting.

Step 3: Present/Clarify the Problem Statement/Session Objective

You will have formulated a Problem Statement/Session Objective before the session. Present it to your group with a minimum of explanation. Give your group a few minutes to "get their hands around it." Using one or two techniques from the Finding Opportunities section in Part 3 gives your group a chance to ask questions and fine tune the statement. Letting them have some control over the direction of the session will enhance their involvement in the process.

Step 4: Generate Ideas

With all the preliminaries out of the way, just say "Go" and let the ideas come pouring out. The process here is to have people speak out any and all of their ideas. If no one seems ready, call on someone to get the ball rolling. Once things heat up your role is to: help clarify ideas; keep the process moving as smoothly as you can; encourage; cajole; ask priming and probing questions; keep the session's goals in mind; adjust to whatever else comes up. You must also work hard to keep judgements and evaluation out of it. Keep it light and fun, but also on track. Not too much to ask, is it?

As your session progresses, you may run into a dry spot. This is not always bad, but don't let it go too long. People begin to think they have run out of ideas when they have only stumbled. A quiet room is not necessarily a dead room. If ideas begin to run dry, pose some new questions. Some possibilities:

- **"Are we yielding to some expected "given" in the problem? What is it and what can we do about it?"**

- **"Are we challenging the obvious?"**

- **"What would a cat do to solve this problem? How about Mel Gibson? A caveman? A child?"**

- **"How would it look from a tree's point of view?"**

These question may expose a new side to the problem and get new ideas flowing. If things grind to a complete halt, go back and turn the problem into an analogy. Think of it as something else: a person, object, or situation. Compare it to a speeding car. Ask how it would look sound, feel, taste as a fat cow. Be inventive. Once you've taken this little excursion, relate it back to the problem and continue using the analogy until a new view of the problem emerges. Proceed from there, looking for new ideas.

Determine in advance either the *length of the session* in time or the *number of ideas* you must generate. At the end of the allotted time or when you reach the goal, either close the session or work toward singling out the most useful ideas. Make this decision before the session begins. Trying to squeeze unplanned activities in at the end of a session leaves everyone feeling dissatisfied.

Nominal Group Technique

The Nominal Group Technique** is a structured, idea-producing process designed to generate ideas in much the same way as classic Brainstorming. The main difference is that initial ideas are generated silently, written down, then reported to the group with no discussion until each participant has reported all of his or her ideas.

The advantage of the Nominal Group Technique is that it allows each participant to assemble her thoughts and ideas before the discussion begins. There is strong research that indicates this technique produces more ideas than Brainstorming. You will find it very useful for groups made up of people reticent to jump in with both feet.

In all its bare simplicity, here's how it works:

Step 1. Silent Idea Generation

The facilitator presents and the group refines the Problem Statement/Session Objective (see Part 3 for more information on how to generate a clear statement/objective). For 10 to 15 minutes, group members write down ideas. Everyone remains silent during this time.

Step 2. Reporting of Ideas

The facilitator moves from person to person around the room gathering ideas one at a time. The facilitator asks each participant for only one idea before moving on to the next person. Each idea is written on the board or large newsprint pad at the front of the room and numbered. The facilitator continues around the room until all ideas have been presented. Participants with multiple ideas (let's hope this includes everyone) present those in successive "rounds." No discussion takes place during this step, but everyone should keep notes of any questions, thoughts, or ideas they get, to be dealt with later.

Step 3. Clarifying and understanding

Once all the ideas have been presented and written down, each is explained. Starting with the first idea and moving down the list, have the person who presented the idea provide more explanation if required. If the information presented is not clear, anyone in the group can ask for clarification. If one idea sounds like another on the list, both ideas should be discussed at that time. The differences between the ideas should be noted.

** Developed by Andre Delbecq and Andrew Van de Ver Veld

Step 4. Ranking

Give the group five–ten minutes to individually review all the ideas. During this time, ask each person to rank the top five ideas he thinks come closest to solving the problem. The best idea receives five points. The next best idea receives four points and so on. Each person reports to the facilitator his choices and the facilitator then puts the corresponding point value beside the idea. To reduce the potential effects of peer pressure, this can be done privately on paper and the totals only recorded on the public record. Once everyone has reported, tally the points. The idea with the most points wins top position. If no clear winner emerges, re-vote, but only on the ideas that received more than three points.

If there is no need to reach a final consensus, everyone can simply list their choices with the ranking number beside it and give this to the facilitator, who can tally the results later.

The Nominal Group Technique is a simple process for generating many ideas in a short period of time. It also offers participants the opportunity to express ideas without having to present them verbally "off the cuff," which can inhibit many people.

The Nominal Group Technique does not develop as much interaction between group members as Brainstorming. If team building is an objective of the session, Brainstorming may be a better choice of techniques.

Attribute Listing

Everything is made up of parts. A pencil for example, has six "hard" parts: the rubber eraser, the metal band, the wood, the paint, the lead (or graphite) and the printing. Other "soft" parts are length, shape, smell, etc. The six hard parts are the primary elements of a pencil.

If you join a group whose charge is to think of ways to improve a pencil, the first thing your mind does is jump into overdrive, because it has been asked to deal with the whole pencil. Hopefully, after a while, your group will settle on one attribute of the pencil, and ideas will start to flow. We have all been in sessions or meetings, however, where this focus never comes, the session wanders aimlessly, and everyone leaves feeling like the time has been wasted. Attribute Listing will help your group quickly and efficiently identify and focus on significant details, leaving you more time and energy to generate good ideas.

Attribute Listing works well as a first step in solving a wide variety of problems. If you are having a problem with an employee, for example, listing as many aspects (or attributes) of the situation as you can will help you understand the problem better. After listing the attributes, look closely at each one to see if it can be modified to solve the problem. Let's say an employee is always late. List all the possible "hard" and "soft" reasons for this lateness—traffic, baby sitter, alarm clock, old car, laziness, low morale—and then choose one area in which to work toward a solution.

It takes focused effort and energy to think of all the attributes of a problem, but finding the right one and working toward modification pays back in multiples. The list you generate will also give you other areas to attack if your initial attempt doesn't fully solve the problem.

Attribute Listing Steps:

1) Have a clear Problem Statement/Session Objective and put it up somewhere in the room where everyone can see it (see Introduction to Problems/Opportunities in Part 3 for more information on this).

2) List all the attributes of the product, object, or problem. For example, a pencil has: rubber eraser, wood, metal band, lead, paint, printing. Brainstorming or another technique can help here.

3) Choose one of these attributes for modification.

4) Use another technique or The Game (Part 5) to help you come up with ideas that can solve the problem.

Attribute Listing is a great way to work your way into a problem and get a look at what may be driving it. Use it all by itself or combine it with other techniques to generate more possible causes and solutions to a problem.

See Sample 1: *The Pencil* in Appendix A to find an example of Attribute Listing combined with Mindmapping and The Game.

Attribute Listing Worksheet *(page 1)*

PROBLEM STATEMENT/SESSION OBJECTIVE:

_____

_____

_____

_____

_____

ATTRIBUTES OF THE PRODUCT, OBJECT, OR PROBLEM:

1. _____

2. _____

3. _____

4. _____

5. _____

6. _____

7. _____

8. _____

9. _____

10. _____

11. _____

12. _____

13. _____

14. _____

15. _____

PROJECT NAME _____   DATE _____ PG. ____ OF ____

Attribute Listing Worksheet *(page 2)*

ATTRIBUTE FOR MODIFICATION

\#_____ _____

Possible Modifications: _____

1. _____

2 _____

3 _____

ATTRIBUTE FOR MODIFICATION

\#_____ _____

Possible Modifications: _____

1. _____

2 _____

3 _____

4. _____

ATTRIBUTE FOR MODIFICATION

\#_____ _____

Possible Modifications: _____

1. _____

2 _____

3 _____

4. _____

5. _____

PROJECT NAME _____   DATE _____ PG. _____ OF _____

Mindmapping

Elephant.

What comes to mind? Big, grey, tusks, circus, peanuts, floppy ears, Dumbo. Your mind did not make a nice neat list of the things that constitute an elephant; no mind does. What the mind does is explode into a whole set of elephantine images that bounce around in total disorder. This is the notion behind Mindmapping, an idea-capturing technique developed by Tony Buzan.

Mindmapping may seem to take you in many different directions before leading you to a solution. It is unique in that it provides a creative maze of thoughts and ideas that can offer new ways to view and explore problems.

When you use this kind of explosion thinking to free ideas without prejudging their worth, you'll be surprised at what comes forth and how productive it can be. During Mindmapping, your flowing thoughts are recorded on paper (never to be lost) and your mind is freed to allow a seamless progression of ideas.

To fully realize the power of Mindmapping, use it often. You'll be amazed at how quickly your mind begins following the winding threads of your creativity.

Mindmapping Steps (it really is this simple):

1) **Start with a key word from your problem or idea and write it in the center of a piece of paper and draw a circle around it. The bigger the paper, the better.**

2) Free your mind to conjure words and images that relate to your center word.

3) **Using the word in the center as a hub, write down those words or draw the images that pop into your head. Connect everything to the center word like the spokes of a wheel.**

4) If one thought sparks another idea or image, draw a line from that word to the new idea or image.

5) **Keep the ideas flowing without any judgement of their worth.**

6) Move freely to any part of the paper and build on any word in any direction that comes to mind. Everything you put down can be traced back, through the lines, to your starting point, so anything goes.

7) **When you run out of ideas, review your mindmap. Group ideas with a common element or which may help solve the problem or which prompt some new way of thinking.**

For instance: If you were going to give a talk on where you find elephants, you would pick out the words that fit this idea and construct your talk around them.

Because the mind thinks with pictures, it is often helpful to draw pictures instead of just using words. While you are drawing, your mind is thinking of new things . . . let them flow and capture everything.

Once you have finished, review your mindmap and assemble your new ideas into a picture or statement. Use this new information as a seed for creativity. Remember the objective is not necessarily to solve a problem but to get everything out and set the mind free to speculate on the information.

A mindmap is a great way to write a report, a novel, review a past meeting, or prepare for the next one. It opens up your mind to new ideas that have been lying there for who knows how long, waiting for the right moment to burst forth. Let your mind have its way with you.

The best way to learn Mindmapping is to do it. It's just that simple.

Elephant Mindmap

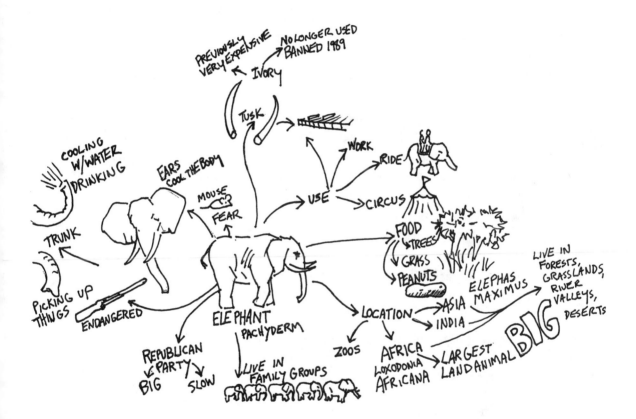

Force-Field Analysis

The Force-Field Analysis, developed by Kurt Lewin in 1947, is a very powerful creative problem-solving tool. The strength of the Force-Field technique stems from its focus on forces already at work in a problem or situation.

The process begins with a detailed analysis of the problem or situation. This analysis leads to discovery of forces already "driving" the problem toward solution and forces "restraining" progress. Once these "driving" and "restraining" forces have been discovered, they are maximized or minimized to generate progress toward solution. The beauty of Force-Field Analysis is that it capitalizes on forces already present within the problem and it breaks the solution down into bite-sized "action steps," easy to chew and swallow.

This "chunking" of the action steps makes Force-Field Analysis ideal for problems which require complex solutions and, therefore, a high degree of cooperation between group members. The Force-Field process calls for detailed action plans involving every member of the group. The completion of the plan as a whole relies heavily on each member accomplishing his or her action steps. The action steps have clearly defined goals and specific, measurable criteria for completion. So, everyone knows when a task has been completed. No if's, maybe's, or excuses. Recognizing and "celebrating" the successes of individuals and ultimately of the group as a whole is an integral part of the Force-Field process.

A Force-Field Analysis is also very flexible. During idea-generating segments, the facilitator can employ a wide range of techniques to get the maximum number of new ideas from the group.

How a Force-Field Analysis works

Pretend your torso is a problem in search of a solution. One of your arms is a rocket, pointing skyward, with a 1000-pound thrust engine blasting away, trying to move your torso up toward solution of the problem. Your other arm is a 1000-pound weight keeping you firmly planted on the ground. As long as these two forces remain equal (in balance), your "torso problem" will remain static with no movement toward solution. Add just one ounce of additional thrust to your rocket, and you slowly begin to rise toward solution. Shed 100 pounds from your weight, and you move more quickly. Add 900 pounds of thrust and shed 500 pounds of weight, and suddenly you are rocketing toward solution.

This is the notion behind a Force-Field Analysis: add power to forces currently working to solve the problem (driving forces) and reduce or eliminate forces which are causing the problem (restraining forces). Sometimes this can be a simple task, other times it will take a real stretch.

Remember one thing: all forces, natural, manmade, and otherwise, are always striving to reach equilibrium, a static state with no movement. You may come up with a solution that will blast your problem into the stratosphere. Bells and whistles sound throughout the land. Be keenly aware, though, that forces in the new situation will work to bring it back to the way it was before you and your hotshot ideas came along.

Vested interest, egos, lethargic thinking and all the rest of it constantly work toward dull, stable, static, status quo stagnation. While your idea is rocketing toward new heights, keep up the thrust. You'll need it when all those who didn't come up with the idea try to bring it back to earth. You may have to give a little to keep your project alive. Dig your heels in when it counts. Don't conquer the dragon, however, only to find you've killed the unicorn in the process.

Following are the steps you'll need to take to conduct your Force-Field Analysis. Be sure to look up the Force-Field sample (Appendix A) and also keep an eye on the worksheets at the end of this section and in Part 6 to help clarify the steps.

In your lust to attack your problem, don't forget about proper warm-ups, appointing a recorder, and setting a comfortable, light, nonjudgmental tone, etc. Review all of Part 2, Setting the Stage, to make your session soar.

Step 1. Analyze the situation and fine tune the Problem Statement/Session Objective.

As you already know from Part 3, developing a clear Problem Statement/Session Objective is critical to finding solutions in any creative process. This is no less true in Force-Field Analysis. Take extra pains to be sure you are addressing the "correct" problem/opportunity. Arrive at your session with a preliminary Problem Statement/Session Objective and have it clearly displayed for everyone to see. Once you have established the basic parameters of your problem/opportunity, there are two steps you can take to bring it into finer focus:

First, examine the current situation and ask some valuable questions.

- **What is happening now that makes this situation a problem?**

- **What has changed recently?**

- **Have new elements have been added?**

- **What new procedures have been implemented?**

- **What new personality is involved that was not there before?**

Using basic Brainstorming principles or the Nominal Group Technique, list everything you can about the current situation and discuss this with your group. In short, determine, "what is."

Second, reverse the point of view and ask:

- **What should be going on?**

- **How would things be if they were the way they should or could be?**

Encourage speculation. It will bring in new perspectives that will be instrumental in setting the stage for creative problem solving later.

These two contrasting views, "what is," and "what should be," will help you formulate your final Problem Statement/Session Objective. Once you have your final statement/objective, put it up on the wall so everyone can see it. For more help with this, go back to Clarifying Opportunities in Part 3 and review some of the techniques on how to be sure you are working on the right problem.

Step 2. List all the forces that are currently driving this problem toward solution (the rocket).

Be sure to list everything, no matter how seemingly insignificant. Remember it only takes an ounce one way or the other to start making a difference.

Step 3. List all the forces at work to keep the problem a problem (the weight).

Again, list everything, especially the things no one wants to talk about. Without them, you'll just be rehashing the same old solutions that haven't worked before. No, it's not easy. Big deal, nothing worth doing is.

Step 4. Review all the forces and have the group determine the most significant driving and restraining forces.

The "most significant" refers to those forces, that, if they could be altered, would have the greatest impact on the problem. Sometimes bringing the group to consensus on the significant forces can be difficult. If you find this, give everyone $100 each for the driving and for the restraining forces ($200 total, figuratively, of course). Have them "spend their money" on their top choices, preferably limiting themselves to four or five, to get some clear indications. One force may get the whole wad. That's OK. Tally the dollars and attack the one with the most first. If there is a tie, have the group respend on just the statements that earned some income in the previous round.

If you feel there may be some political or peer pressure in the room and want to really capture everyone's independent opinions, a private spending structure might work best. Simply have each group member write the number of the idea with the dollar amount next to it on a slip of paper. This also keeps everyone honest in how much they spend.

Step 5. Re-state the chosen force(s) into Problem Statement(s)/Session(s) Objective(s).

Remember to phrase these in ways that establish clear direction and invite participation. Example: change "Figure out how to speed up paperwork" to "Find five ways to reward anyone who beats a reporting deadline." For more information on this, see Part 3, Finding Opportunities.

Step 6: Start the creative idea-generating portion of your session.

In this step you have many choices. To begin generating ideas, you can use any of the techniques presented earlier in this section, The Game (Part 5), or any of a multitude of other techniques outside the scope of this book (look around; they're out there). Everything is acceptable. There are no rights or wrongs, but sometimes one method is better than another.

Step 7. Once you have ideas the group thinks will solve the problem, test each one or all of them together with a BenBalance (Part 6) or another assessment technique.

Don't forget good ideas never die; they are alive and malleable. If and when you discover weaknesses in your best ideas, modify them, patch them, build on them, expand them. You'll find they only get stronger as a result of all this twisting, prodding, and poking.

Step 8. List all the actions needed to achieve the goal on the Specific Actions Page (Part 6).

Again, minutiae are essential. O-rings brought down the space shuttle and a potential Indy 500 champion. Almost nothing is too minute to deserve your attention. List it. You can cross it off later.

Step 9. Determine the duties, resources, and timing on the Resources Page (Part 6).

Always put one person's name in the PERSON slot. If an action step requires a committee, put the name of the chairperson. If two people are involved, either break the task up or choose one to take responsibility. Without responsibility, you might as well be playing croquet.

Step 10. List your completion criteria on the Celebration Document (Part 6).

Be very specific when listing your completion criteria. If the task is to get a phone installed, the completion criterion is "make a phone call." Settle for nothing less. Hold everyone to their commitments. If someone hasn't completed his task, wait until it gets done to proceed. And, when it gets done, CELEBRATE IT!!

These are the steps in a Force-Field Analysis. They won't all be easy. Things can, and do go wrong; someone will have a "great" idea and be willing to defend it to the death, reaching consensus on the most powerful forces might take hours, or you might forget to consider an important force and need to rethink the whole project. Not one of these problems, however, can ever be as detrimental to the creative process as working without some structure, the kind of structure the Force-Field process provides.

The most amazing thing about Force-Field Analysis is that when it comes to assigning actions, most of the time people will volunteer. If they don't, just say, "OK, picking up the hot dogs? Mary, could you do that?" You will almost never hear a "no."

In the right hands, your hands, the Force-Field Analysis is a powerful tool that will produce a myriad of valuable and often inexpensive solutions. Use it well and it will repay you in a wealth of accomplishments.

Force-Field Analysis Worksheet *(page 1)*

SITUATION STATEMENT

_____

_____

Forces driving this situation toward solution:

_____

_____

_____

_____

_____

_____

_____

_____

_____

_____

Forces restraining success in this situation:

_____

_____

_____

_____

_____

_____

_____

_____

_____

_____

PROJECT NAME _____   DATE _____ PG. _____ OF _____

69

Force-Field Analysis Worksheet *(page 2)*

MOST SIGNIFICANT DRIVING FORCE*

_____

_____

_____

_____

Statement/Objective to strengthen driving force:

_____

_____

_____

_____

MOST SIGNIFICANT RESTRAINING FORCE*

_____

_____

_____

_____

Statement/Objective to weaken restraining force:

_____

_____

_____

_____

Based on estimated return for effort.

PROJECT NAME _____   DATE _____ PG. _____ OF _____

© FLOYD HURT 1999 1 (800) THINK NU

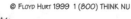

70

PART 5

The Game

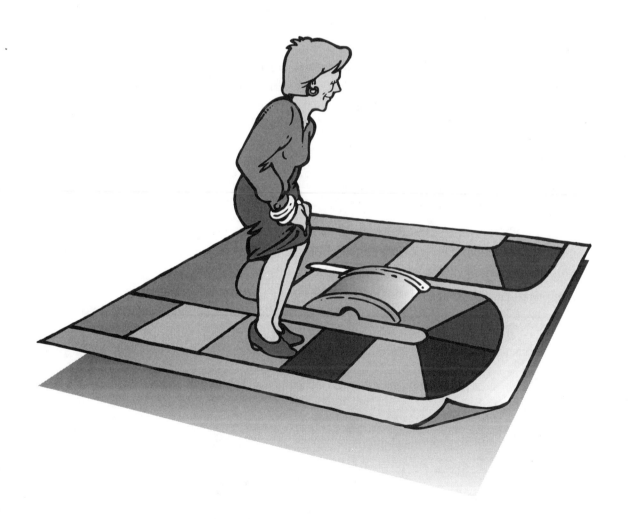

Introduction to The Game

You've read. You've learned. You've studied. You've practiced. Now it's time to play.

How many times have you been asked to "think up something new," without any clear guidelines? This "freedom" is supposed to allow you to be more creative, right? Wrong. Without any limitations, you are being asked to think of the whole world. Because you don't know where to start, you spend a great deal of time wandering around looking for the spark to get things going or provide a fresh point of view. The Game provides this spark.

Far too often people sit in a creative session and are reticent to offer ideas "out of the blue" because of the risk involved. The Game, through its random selection of "creative prompts," puts everyone into the same "out-of-the blue" boat. This "creative equality" makes participants less self-conscious and more willing to get involved and present their far-out ideas. The Game, as a result, sets a tone and a provides a forum conducive to creativity, past the edge of the expected.

Because creativity is often found in the unfamiliar, you often need to turn things upside down or inside out to get an unfamiliar perspective. The Game prompts you to explore the unfamiliar by providing you with a wide range of stimuli. These stimuli force your mind to leap outside everyday boundaries. The Game pushes you beyond the ordinary, beyond the already known.

How does The Game accomplish all this? It does so by providing the "players" with a wide variety of creative prompts. These prompts force new perspectives and new mind-sets. The prompts are collected into seven lists:

- **Aspects of the Problem**

- **Verb Commands**

- **Objects**

- **Heroes**

- **Picture This**

- **Use your Senses**

- **Game Break**

The facilitator chooses the most appropriate "Creative Prompt List," and, through a random number selection process, the "players" are prompted to look at a problem, situation, product, etc. from a new perspective.

For example, if a session were focusing on the problem of too much traffic in the copy room in the morning, the facilitator might choose the Heroes Creative Prompt List. Through a simple process, the number "3" comes up. Hero number 3 is Mahatma Ghandi. The group must now decide how Mahatma Ghandi might view this problem and the ideas he might have to solve it. This kind of shift requires everyone to bring a brand new point of view to the situation; one that allows them to escape from themselves and play with a new persona. Some ideas might arise like: "Have a silent protest." This may yield: put some chairs outside the copy room and everyone shifts seats toward the copy room each time someone leaves. "Boycott the copy room." This may force management to buy a new machine. "Go on a hunger strike." Provide an incentive if copying is done during lunch. "Meditate." Decide if that copy is really necessary.

Using Mahatma Ghandi has given the group a focal point around which to pile their now unusual ideas. These are not necessarily the ideas that will directly solve the problem, but by getting outside the ordinary and the expected, the group expands its horizons and moves toward a truly innovative solution which may not have been found by traditional methods.

The object of The Game is to force everyone to view a problem or situation from an entirely new perspective. By moving away from the expected, you think unexpectedly. Remember, creativity often requires taking the unfamiliar and making it familiar or combining unrelated ideas and/or objects.

The Game is not a trivial add-on to this book which you can skip over. It is not to be saved for rare spare time. In fact, The Game is an essential component of this entire creative enterprise. All that you have experienced up to this point has been leading you here. Trust in the power of The Game and allow yourself the freedom to make it work for you. Keep playing, no matter how zany the ideas become. Explore the ridiculous and embrace the absurd. You will be amazed at the practical, usable results you'll ultimately produce.

The keys to The Game's success are your own mind's freedom, your willingness to take risks, the random selection of the creative prompts, and a capable facilitator to guide you. Each "player" needs to be completely at ease with wild ideas, strange notions, flights of fancy, and unexpected releases from dark taboos. Keeping the selection of the creative prompts random eliminates the possibility of finger pointing when a group faces a particularly challenging task. Don't underestimate the negative effects this finger pointing can have on your session.

Rule 1: Censor nothing . . . NOTHING.

Rule 2: Everything stays in the room unless agreed otherwise.

Rule 3: Have fun. After all, it's only a game.

The Game Uses

The Game has one driving purpose: to help you find "outside the expected" ideas for identifying opportunities and solving problems.

The ultimate beauty of The Game is its spin-off of usefulness. Once you have mastered the basic principles, you'll find them creeping quietly into places you never thought they could go.

The first and most obvious use of The Game is as its own self-contained, idea-generating/problem-solving session. Once you have a clear Problem Statement/Session Objective (see Part 3, Finding Opportunities), you can play The Game pretty much straight up. Just don't forget to follow all the basic principles of a productive creative session (avoid criticism, appoint a recorder, etc.).

The second most logical use of The Game is as a major section in another problem-solving session, such as a Force-Field Analysis. Step 6 of the Force-Field process asks you to "start the creative, idea-generating portion of your session." A few rounds of The Game would be a perfect way to help get the ideas flowing.

Thirdly, The Game can be inserted more inconspicuously into sessions such as Brainstorming or the Nominal Group Technique. At the critical creative moments in those sessions, when the group members have been asked to generate new ideas, a quick round or two of The Game can get people loosened up and offer huge payoffs.

Finally comes the most subtle use of The Game. This occurs informally as a simple question you might ask in a session or in everyday conversation. Asking a colleague, "How is this problem like golf?" (from the Object Stretch list) might help her find a new angle on a problem. Suggesting, "make it fragile" (from the Verb Command list) to someone who is trying to get a better understanding of a problem could trigger ideas which might not come out in other ways.

This last use of The Game is entirely informal, and, because it can catch people off guard, you must employ it judiciously. Remember, not everyone is wide open to these unique approaches. But, you'll find as you learn how to use them, people will begin to search you out "to help them think." Your reputation as someone who gets the most out of people will grow rapidly, and who knows what else will grow with it.

Pre-Game Preparations

There are some things to consider before you play The Game. Many of these have been explained in detail earlier in this book.

For your Game session to be most successful, you will need an effective facilitator. The facilitator should review the Guidelines for Facilitators in Part 2. A good facilitator directs the group without dominating or squelching the process. This is a delicate balance which takes practice to master.

For the most effective and productive session, players should read this entire book before beginning. If that is not possible, then, at a minimum, have each player read Guidelines to Participants (Part 2) and all of Part 5, The Game. This will smooth the session by getting everyone on a solid footing.

To get the very most from the players and the session, supply each player with a copy of this book. When new ideas start cropping up all over the place, you'll find this a profitable investment.

Another issue you want to resolve before the session begins is the seating plan. This is an important consideration in getting the most out of the session. If your session is going to have more than eight players, you should break into sub-groups. Running the session with sub-groups has some distinct advantages:

- **It multiplies the potential number of ideas.**

- **Smaller groups are less likely to get side-tracked onto side points.**

- **It enhances the involvement of every player.**

- **Players are usually less concerned about expressing their zany thoughts to a smaller, more intimate group.**

- **In a sub-group, players are less likely to abstain from contributing. Silence in a group of 12 or 15 is invisible. In a group of five, it is obvious.**

The optimal number of players for a highly productive sub-group is five or six.

Because there are many advantages to sub-groups, the instructions from here on assume their use.

Pre-game Preparations:

1) Decide on the Creative Prompt List(s) you will use in the session. At the session, each sub-group should have only one copy of the book. If you end up with several copies per sub-group, have only one on the table. This helps keep the players focused and not reading.

2) Organize the room so members of sub-groups can face each other and easily work together. Also be sure no one has his back to the front of the room, so everyone can easily see the facilitator.

3) Be sure there is plenty of paper and a pencil for each participant.

4) Once your participants have gathered, follow the procedures for any good creative session (see Part 2, Setting the Stage). Unless everyone knows each other well, supply name cards (5" x 8" index cards folded to stand up work well).

5) Welcome everyone to the session and have the players introduce themselves.

6) Appoint a sub-facilitator for each sub-group. An easel with large newsprint pad for each sub-group can help them be more productive.

7) Perform a warm-up exercise such as listing as many things as you can do with a paper clip. This is done within the sub-groups both to establish the routine and to get the groups oiled up.

8) Present the Problem Statement/Session Objective. The first round(s) of the game will most likely be focused on clarifying this statement.

Now that you are all set-up, oiled-up, and psyched-up, you're ready to PLAY!

Playing The Game

Once all your preparations have been made, the tables are set, the sub-groups are formed, the sub-facilitators and other roles assigned, the Problem Statement/Session Objective presented, and the warm-up completed, it's time to PLAY. Let the games BEGIN!

Here's how it works. The rest of this chapter contains the seven "Creative Prompt Lists":

1. Aspects of the Problem

2. Verb Commands

3. Objects

4. Heroes

5. Picture This

6. Use your Senses

7. Game Break

Each list is composed of creative prompts which help you clarify problems, generate ideas, or find solutions to problems. Each list is preceded by a detailed explanation of its features and how to use it. Be sure to read these explanations carefully before your session so you can use the lists effectively during the game.

When you have determined which list you'll be using, follow these steps to play The Game:

1) Note how many items are in the list you have selected for this round.

2) Ask each player to write down three numbers between one and (the number of items in the list) on a scrap of paper and put these into a pile at the center of the table.

3) Have the sub-facilitators pick out three numbers from the pile. These are the numbers of the Creative Prompts from the list that the group will use. It is usually best to have each sub-group choose three prompts at a time.

4) Have the sub-groups look up their numbers in the appropriate Creative Prompt List.

5) Before setting the sub-groups to work, the facilitator checks to see if there are any questions.

6) Have the sub-groups open their discussion by deciding which of the three prompts the group wants to start with and focus on. Remind them they can always return to the others if they run aground.

7) Set a time limit and put the groups to work.

8) When the working time is up, each sub-group reports its ideas. Have one person from each sub-group stand and present their ideas. Avoid long explanations. Allow questions for clarification. Promote "hitchhiking." Encourage good-natured laughter. Avoid criticism or judgement. Have everyone take notes and/or have a recorder write up the ideas in front of the whole group.

9) Once all the ideas have been presented, play additional rounds of the game if necessary.

10) When time is running down, you can review ideas, classify them, judge them, discuss them, or perform some other kind of analysis. This depends on the objective of your session.

Some reminders:

- Write ideas down.

- Start with a warm up exercise.

- Be sure your problem is clear and you have an objective for the session.

- Above all, set a tone which will not tolerate criticism, put-downs, or finger pointing.

And now it's on with the show!! Read the introductions to each prompt list carefully and have a blast!

#1 Aspects of the Problem, Introduction Numbers 1–10

The unspoken, the unaddresed, the assumed and a host of other tacit aspects of a problem or situation can preclude the best creative output from an individual or a group. This Prompt List is designed to illuminate these often unaddressed points and bring them into the open for discussion. If everyone is not truthful and up-front with answers to these questions, the final solution will be a patch, not a full solution.

The strength of this list is its ability to clarify the essence of a problem. This is critical because without a clearly focused problem, there is little chance of finding a solution.

As you read the questions in the list, you'll notice that if they are answered honestly, some volatile information is likely to come out. Confidentiality, therefore, is essential in making this exercise productive. It is imperative that what is said stay in the room. If word gets out that ol' Joe brought up a shocking subject, ol' Joe won't trust the group, nor will the other members. Your group will disintegrate . . . KEEP IT IN THE ROOM AT ALL COSTS.

You may find your session spending more time here than intended. This is not always bad. You may even find that you want to attack all ten of these prompts because of the discussion and information they initiate. If the facilitator decides to cover all ten questions, she could put the numbers 1–10 in a hat and have each sup-group draw out two or three. Remember to keep the selections random.

Recommendations:

1) Emphasize confidentiality.

2) Don't let the reporting phase turn into a gripe session. You do want to bring out concerns, dissatisfaction, frustrations, but always with an eye toward how they can be fixed. Don't let the group wallow in self-pity. You are here to overcome that.

Note to facilitator:

As the facilitator, you are seeking information to help open up thinking and further the understanding of the problem. If something is unclear, ask for clarifications or amplification. If you feel people are holding back, you may be right. Every organization has skeletons that are not allowed out of the closet. If you meet too much resistance on an issue, let it go. You can't solve all the problems, and you may end up making everyone edgy. It can be beneficial to point out the resistance you are feeling and encourage everyone to explore why it exists. Don't ask for an answer to the issue, just an awareness that it exists. Answers may be for another time.

#1 Aspects of the Problem Prompt List, Numbers 1–10**

1) What aspects of this situation are we trying to dodge and why?
There are "hot buttons," political demons and hidden undercurrents everyone avoids. Address these no-no's and you'll open your options.

2) What factors are essential, driving, and paramount? Why are they essential? Are they real?
Some aspects of the problem or situation can't be avoided. You need to know what they are, but also understand they are NOT limitations. All "essential" factors should be considered suspect. Be sure not to let them become controlling factors . . . that misses the point of the session.

3) What limitations do we face, are they real, and why?
In the "creative" part of the session, there are no limitations. In the real world, there may be. By discussing these limitations you will start questioning their causes and validity . . . often a taboo subject. You will also force the group to think about ways to attack the limits. Under no circumstances should these limitations hamper thinking or restrict options. It should force everyone to think even more creatively.

4) What are the hidden agendas? Who has them, and why?
Not everyone will agree with your group or the process. The boss may have an agenda no one talks about. It needs to be addressed, or things can come to a standstill. Remember, confidentiality is paramount when discussing these points.

5) What assumptions are we making and why?
Assumptions are just that . . . question them for validity. Times change, assumptions crumble.

6) Who will we have to convince, and what do they think now?
Provide this information by name and position. Remember, you have to sell the idea. It helps to know what or who you are up against.

7) What would we have to do to make the problem worse?
This is a great way to help determine where the problem resides. Make it worse and you'll discover what makes it bad in the first place. This kind of footing will provide a terrific starting point for attack.

8) If we don't solve this problem, what will happen?
This can help you isolate forces that will bring you toward solution. Ask also: Who or what will be affected if the problem continues, and how?

9) What solutions could we never accept? Why? What would happen if we suggested them? Can they be modified so they'll work?
This kind of thinking provides insight into the unthinkable. Remember, creative ideas must TRANSCEND the natural order of things. These questions compel this kind of thinking.

**A great deal of work has been done in this area by Edward DeBono. His books are available almost everywhere

10) What are some things that could hold back this session and why?
Fear of retribution, uneven participation, fear of making a fool of ourselves . . . recognize limitations and then overcome them.

#2 Verb Commands, Introduction Numbers 1–140

Verbs are creative magic. Ask someone to come up with ideas to improve a product or service and you have given them too much to think about; the mind pauses in confusion. Give them a verb command such as: "Put it to music," or "Make it a Collector's Item," and the mind assembles new and different pictures to solve the problem. This is the notion behind the Verb Command Creative Prompt List.

This list's greatest strength is its ability to get the players to see new aspects of and potential in a problem or situation. It takes imagination and is often a good place to start or a good choice for a quick round of The Game as part of another kind of session.

Before setting the sub-groups to work, the facilitator or sub-facilitator should prime the pump with some questions about the command:

Example: Verb command # 52 is "Make it Unrealistic."

The facilitator might ask: "What does the term 'unrealistic' mean?" "Name some things you (address one person in the group) consider unrealistic and why." "What makes something unrealistic?" "What is the most unrealistic thing you can think of?" etc.

Recommendations:

1) In a few extra minutes of work time, have the sub-groups choose one of the three verb commands from which to force a solution to the problem.

2) Be sure to keep the sub-groups' reports concise. You might decide to allow the sub-groups to report only on one verb command. This forms important consensus building skills and avoids overwhelming the whole group with too many ideas.

3) If a sub-group doesn't feel it can work with the verb commands it has selected and likes other ones better, the facilitator must make a difficult choice. Don't let the players off the hook too easily. Remember, being creative is hard work that takes discipline. If the group is allowed to run out of gas too easily, it will miss the opportunity to expand its thinking. However, it will do no good to alienate the players. Be firm, but flexible.

#2 Verb Command Prompt List, Number 1–140

1. Make it bigger
2. Make it smaller
3. Make it tiny
4. Make it round
5. Make it square
6. Make it longer
7. Make it shorter
8. Make it sparkle
9. Make it light up
10. Make it heavier
11. Make it lighter
12. Make it weightless
13. Enclose it
14. Fill it up
15. Empty it
16. Coil it
17. Open it
18. Put it in a bottle, can, box
19. Turn it upside down
20. Lay it on its side
21. Stretch it
22. Shrink it
23. Change its color
24. Make it visual
25. Put it into words
26. Put it to music
27. Eliminate words
28. Eliminate pictures
29. Make it clamorous
30. Silence it
31. Use repetition
32. Make it two-dimensional
33. Change the shape
34. Change a part
35. Make it a set

36. Make it a collector's item
37. Mechanize it
38. Electrify it
39. Make it move
40. Reverse it
41. Make it look like something else
42. Give it texture
43. Make it romantic
44. Add nostalgic appeal
45. Make it look old-fashioned
46. Make it look futuristic
47. Make it part of something else
48. Make it stronger
49. Make it fragile
50. Make it durable
51. Use symbolism
52. Be unrealistic
53. Use a new art style
54. Make it cooler
55. Make it hotter
56. Change the scent
57. Make it appeal to children
58. Make it appeal to women
59. Make it appeal to men
60. Change one ingredient
61. Add new ingredients
62. Twist it
63. Make it transparent
64. Make it opaque
65. Glamorize it
66. Use another material
67. Add human interest

68. Change the package
69. Make it compact
70. Miniaturize it
71. Eliminate it
72. Maximize it
73. Make it portable
74. Make it collapsible
75. Go to extremes
76. Summarize it
77. Winterize it
78. Personalize it
79. Make it darker
80. Make it shine
81. Make it grow up
82. Split it
83. Understate it
84. Exaggerate it
85. Make it a substitute
86. Find a new use for it
87. Subtract it
88. Add it
89. Divide it
90. Use the obvious
91. Lower it
92. Raise it
93. Isolate it
94. Speed it up
95. Slow it down
96. Make it fly
97. Pulverize it
98. Put sex appeal into it
99. Condense it
100. Bend it
101. Match it
102. Suspend it
103. Make it stand upright
104. Make it lay flat

105. Make it symmetrical
106. Make it asymmetrical
107. Sharpen it
108. Change its contour
109. Nickname it
110. Concentrate it
111. Spread it out
112. Solidify it
113. Liquefy it
114. Soften it
115. Harden it
116. Make it narrow
117. Make it wider
118. Make it funny/silly
119. Make it satirical
120. Find a second use for it
121. Sell it as a kit
122. Purify it
123. contaminate it
124. Fold it
125. Unfold it
126. Extend it
127. Add comfort to it
129. Make it uncomfortable
130. Use a different texture
131. Sweeten it
132. Make it sour
133. Moisten it
134. Freeze it
135. Make it slapstick
136. Extrude it
137. Make it irrational
138. Give it eye appeal
139. Give it ear appeal
140. Make it glow

#3 Object Stretch, Introduction Numbers 1–100

The purpose of the Object Stretch list is to stimulate a discussion of how an object is similar to the problem you are attacking, or how you might use an object to solve the problem.

You may have in-depth knowledge of the object, or you may have no idea what it is or what it does. Either way is OK. It may take a great deal of mind stretching to relate the Aswan Dam to a specific problem. That's why you do it. When you think about the object, don't limit your thinking to just what it is or what it does. Consider everything that relates to that object. For example, the Aswan Dam generates electricity; it has an overflow; it floods the land behind it; it is built of massive amounts of concrete; there are fish in the lake; it is in Egypt, where the Pharaohs lived. You need to consider how any or all of this is like the problem, or how it can be used to solve the problem. The only limit to the possibilities of any object is the limit of your imagination.

The strength of this list is its ability to force new, uncharted approaches to a problem. Finding an analogy for your problem or situation might be difficult and require some imaginative gymnastics. That's why it's worth doing.

Recommendations:

1) Remind the players that the discussion should center on how the problem is like the object. Caution them not to get sidetracked into a discussion of the object, unless it is leading them to an analogy.

2) If a group feels it can't work with the selected object, be firm but flexible. Don't let the players off the hook too easily. Remember, being creative is hard work that takes discipline.

#3 Object Stretch Prompt List, Numbers 1–100

1. Aswan High Dam
2. Teeth
3. Atomic Bomb
4. Gasoline-Fueled Engine
5. Tower of Babel
6. Butterfly
7. Chameleon
8. Dinosaur
9. Earthworm
10. Monkey
11. Computer
12. Barometer
13. Everglades
14. Evolution
15. Clock
16. Eye
17. Food Chain
18. Galaxy
19. Television
20. Chemical Warfare
21. Magnet
22. Police
23. Digestive System
24. Gettysburg Address
25. Electricity
26. Golf
27. Grafting
28. CIA
29. Casablanca (the movie)
30. Group Psychotherapy
31. Sponge
32. Gyroscope
33. Heart
34. Hieroglyphic
35. Brain

36. Iceberg
37. Infantry
38. Gun Powder
39. Radar
40. Broadway
41. Glacier
42. Sailboat
43. Irrigation
44. Telephone
45. Gymnastics
48. IRS
48. Jet
48. Knitting
49. Marines
50. Greenhouse Effect
51. Mosaic
52. Ship in a Bottle
53. Guide Dog
54. Muscles
55. Camel
56. Library
57. Music
58. Natural Selection
59. Circulatory System
60. Nervous System
61. Onion
62. Bermuda Triangle
63. Orchestra
64. Parasite
65. Congress
66. Parrot
67. Billiards
68. Gear
69. Planetarium
70. Morse Code

71. Stomach
72. Pottery
73. Lungs
74. Geometry
75. Ocean
76. Respiration
77. Scuba Diving
78. Generator
79. Solar System
80. Submarine
81. Olympic Games
82. Sundial
83. Tapestry
84. Ballet
85. Taxidermy
86. Tornado
87. Sewing Machine
88. Tunnel
89. Velcro
90. Waste Disposal
91. Mythology
92. Windmill
93. Skeleton
94. Wind Tunnel
95. Mill Wheel
96. Sex
97. Cloud
98. Gravitation
99. Acting
100. Language

#4 Heroes, Introduction
Numbers 1–35

What if you could tap into the creativity, talents, or reputation of anyone in the world from any time period to help solve a problem? The Heroes Prompt List allows you to do just that. The goal of this list is to introduce new, imaginative thinking and add a little excitement by having a hero solve the problem.

The strength of this list is that it provides a distinct persona from which to gain new perspectives. It challenges the players to take entirely alien views of the problem or situation.

Before you start, tell everyone to get out of their own head and become the "Hero" they'll be learning about. Ask them to think about how this hero would solve the problem, not themselves. What special talents or expertise would he/she bring to this situation. Read the information blurb about the "Hero." When you finish, ask if anyone has anything to add. If a player knows nothing about this character, it's all right. Lie. It adds a new dimension and makes it more fun. Let misunderstanding and confusion be your guide, it will take you into uncharted lands.

Recommendations:

1) Encourage players to go a little wild by having them assume the character(s)' identity and present the information in character.

2) Two players can assume character identities and present the information in a dialogue or as a debate.

3) Encourage players to use the body language, the accent and the gestures of the hero. It is amazing how free we are when we assume a new persona.

4) Facilitators should continue to be firm yet flexible in letting sub-groups change their selection from one hero to another. The point is to "force" the process, not give in to difficulties.

#4 Heroes Prompt List, Numbers 1–35

1. *Harry Houdini:* A magician and escape artist. He could escape from any kind of bond or container. He could free himself from handcuffs, shackles, straightjackets or other devices even while under water or in midair. He always told his friends that after he died, he would come back.

2. *Lucille Ball:* An accomplished, effervescent comedienne with red hair, a rasping voice and a Latin husband named Ricky. She had perfect timing in all of her comedic actions. Think of the candy factory where the candies came at her faster than she could deal with them.

3. *Mahatma Gandhi:* The preeminent leader of Indian nationalism. He lived his life by jettisoning material goods (money and property) that cramped the life of the spirit. He also remained unmoved by pain or pleasure, victory or defeat. One of his major ways of protesting was to fast.

4. *Yogi Berra:* Baseball player, catcher, and coach. Played with New York Yankees including 14 World Series. His most famous quote: "It ain't over 'til it's over."

5. *Marilyn Monroe:* Beautiful, sexy, "dumb blonde" actress. Had a flair for light comedy. Starred in, "How to Marry a Millionaire," "Gentleman Prefer Blondes," "Some Like it Hot." Let your mind go with: "Happy Birthday, Mr. President."

6. *Henry Ford:* Industrialist and pioneer automobile manufacturer. He conceived the modern assembly-line mass productions for manufacturing the famous Model-T Ford. "I'll give the public any color they want, as long as it's black."

7. *Robin Hood:* Legendary outlaw who lived in Sherwood Forest with his band of Merry Men. He protected the poor by outwitting, robbing, and killing the rich and giving the money to the poor. He had a big sidekick named Little John.

8. *Bacchus:* Greek and Roman god of wine, vegetation, and fertility. He is the father of the Bacchanalia, an orgiastic and drunken celebration. Bacchus experimented with grapes that grew on Mount Nysa, and made a drink unknown to all, even the gods. He sampled it to the point where the nymphs thought he had gone mad.

9. *Xena, The Warrior Princess:* Daughter of our post-modern fascination with the distant past and the unknown future, Xena combines cartooninsh qualities with real flesh-and-blood guts and courage. Whether wielding a battle sword, chasing "bad guys," or just generally carousing around the misty medieval countryside, Xena captures the imagination. How does she stay on that horse anyway?

10. *Eros:* Mythological god of Bringing Together. He is armed with a bow that shoots arrows of love and passion into suitable and often unsuitable couples. He became a confidant of Venus/Aphrodite and sat watching her and Ares "at play" in the hay.

11. *Odysseus:* Mythological hero of antiquity and of the Trojan War. He was a major military figure and is credited with the idea of the wooden horse. After the war he took the long way home and had adventurers with the Cyclops, a one-eyed giant, whom he blinded with a hot stick, and the Sirens, nymphs whose song lured men to shipwreck. He lashed himself to the mast so he would not be tempted.

12. *Rosa Parks:* Unintentional symbol and leader of the civil rights movement. "Little" Rosa Parks refused to give up her seat in the front of the bus after a tiring day at work and sparked the public-transit boycott which ended segregation, at least on the busses in her city.

13. *Zeus:* Sovereign Lord of Olympus. He gained the earth after the battle of the Titans. The underworld went to Hades, the sea to Poseidon, and the earth to Zeus. He was a lustful god, taking his pleasure with goddesses, nymphs, and mortals. His frequent affairs with mortals were carried out when Zeus changed into an animal. Europa was taken by a bull, Ganymede by an eagle, both Zeus incognito. He inflicted terrible punishment on offenders. When Prometheus stole fire from Olympus, Zeus secured him to a rock for 30,000 years and sent an eagle to feed on his liver every day.

14. *W. C. Fields:* Actor who ran away to become a vaudeville actor and juggler. A bulbous nose and gravelly voice helped his image, maybe real, as a child- and pet-hating misanthrope. This is the man who said, "a man who hates dogs and children can't be all bad."

15. *Harriet Tubman:* Legendary "founder" of the Underground Railroad, this folk hero is remembered for her bravery, tenacity, and indomitable spirit in the face of seemingly insurmountable odds.

16. *Martin Luther King:* Civil rights leader and brilliant orator. He galvanized the civil rights movement based on the principle of non-violence. His most memorable oration was the "I have a dream" speech delivered in Washington.

17. *Huck Finn:* A fictitious character created by Mark Twain. Huck and his friends Jim and Tom sail down the Mississippi river from adventure to adventure. He spends a great deal of time scorning respectability and dealing in petty thievery. He is a "bad boy" with lots of good.

18. *Nicolaus Copernicus:* Astronomer. His work questioned the existing notion of the solar system where it was assumed the earth was its center. He challenged the existing belief of the church's heliocentric system and proved that the earth was only a minor player.

19. *Lady Godiva:* Her possibly true attempt to get her husband to lift a tax on his subjects by riding naked down Main Street has been transformed into the story of a long-haired, demure lady calmly and nakedly riding her horse through the village. Supposedly, Peeping Tom was the only one to take a peek (Lady G. had asked all residents to stay indoors and shut their windows), and he was struck blind.

20. *Pablo Picasso:* A great artistic innovator. His work is divided into three primary periods: the blue period, showing a series of striking studies of the poor and those in despair, the pink period of life-affirming harlequins, acrobats, and circus life, and the brown period, where he worked in sculpture. In almost every way, he broke with tradition.

21. *Walt Disney:* American film producer and a pioneer in animated cartoons. He could bring to life almost anything, including a little mouse named Mickey. He opened gargantuan amusement parks. There was always some concern about Disney talking about his ideas, for fear of someone stealing them. "I can think them up faster than they can copy them," he said.

22. *Dorothy:* Media darling to generations of viewers. Dorothy joins the Scarecrow, Tin Man and Lion in defeating the Wicked Witch in order to receive their just rewards. Dorothy's most admirable characteristic: bringing out the best in others.

23. *Albert Einstein:* A theoretical physicist with a really big brain. His theories about the atom led to the atomic bomb . . . $E = MC^2$. His special Theory of Relativity dealt with systems of observers in uniform (unaccelerated) motion with respect to one another. He was working on a unified field theory tying together subatomic phenomena and large-scale phenomena under one set of laws.

24. *Marie Curie:* French physicist. She and her husband worked on magnetism and radioactivity (a term she invented). She isolated radium and polonium. She and her husband were awarded the Nobel Prize for physics.

25. *Joan of Arc:* Powerful contributor to the liberation of France from English tyranny in the 15th century. St. Joan broke with all tradition by becoming a warrior, and a good one, leading her compatriots in raising the siege of Orleans and conducting Charles VII to his coronation. She was handed over to the English, who sentenced her as a heretic and burned her.

26. *Hannibal:* Carthaginian soldier whose father made him swear eternal enmity to Rome. He fought many battles against the Romans, but the most remembered is his famous trip across the Alps in the Second Punic War. He set out with a full train of baggage, men, and elephants and then overran the Po valley.

27. *Niccolo Machiavelli:* Italian statesman, writer, and political philosopher. With the return of the Medici family to Florence, Machiavelli was sent to prison and tortured. Later pardoned, he turned to writing. His most famous work is *The Prince.* In this book, he states that, "the ends justify the means." In short, do what it takes to get the job done, because no matter how bad it is, it is not as bad as what they can do to you.

28. *Helen:* "The face that launched 1000 ships." To resolve a dispute in the heavens, Helen is "given" to Paris. When read carefully, though, questions arise as to how strongly Helen resisted. She proves fickle and even tries to trick her rescuers (hidden in the Trojan Horse) into revealing themselves.

29. *Laurel and Hardy:* American comedy team. Their routine was built around good, honest slapstick, with no attempt to be subtle. Hardy was fat, pretentious, and blustering. He played with his tie and often turned to the audience for help. Laurel was thin, often bullied, and confused. When confused, he scratched his head and cried. They pushed a piano out of a window.

30. *Calvin & Hobbes:* A very mischievous boy and his tiger. When adults are around, Hobbes is a lifeless stuffed animal. When he is with Calvin, he is alive and talkative. Calvin is a regular "bad boy." He has a transmogrifier that can change a cardboard box into a spaceship.

31. *Jesse Jackson:* American politician with a firebrand form of oratory. He is a charismatic preacher and very determined black activist. He formed the "Rainbow Coalition" of minority social and political groups.

32. *Janus:* mythological custodian of the universe and god of beginnings. He is represented with two faces looking in opposite directions because he knew both the past and the future. The month of January is named after him because it is the bridge between the old year and the new.

33. *Alexander Graham Bell:* Inventor of the telephone. For many years he studied and experimented with speech and teaching people to speak. As early as 1865, he thought about sending voice by wire. In 1876, he perfected the first telephone. His first words were: "Mr. Watson, come here."

34. *Daniel Boone:* American pioneer and explorer. He was the first to explore Kentucky as an agent for the Transylvania Company. He blazed the Wilderness Road and founded Boonesboro, KY. Many of his legends were of his own making and later disproved. He did know how to spin a tale.

35. *Buddha:* The enlightened one. A philosopher. He left a life of luxuries and a beautiful wife to become an ascetic. He sat under a banyan tree and conceived the answer to life in the "four noble truths:" life is suffering; the cause of suffering is desire; there is a cessation of suffering called Nirvana or total transcendence; and there is a path leading to the end of suffering, the "eightfold noble path" of right views, right resolve, right speech, right action, right livelihood, right effort, right mindfulness, and right concentration.

#5 Picture This, Introduction Numbers 1–30

One picture is worth a thousand ideas.

The set of photographs included in this section are random shots with no particular meaning. What they could be is something else . . . that's up to you. As you look at them, let your mind wander and speculate.

There are two ways to use the photos. The first way is to have the group determine how the problem is like one of the photographed items (similar to the Object Stretch List). If the number "23" comes up, ask how the problem is like some item in the photograph, the steam locomotive, lawn chairs, railroad tracks, telephone pole, smoke, hats. This will open new discussion of the problem and prompt an entirely new kind of thinking.

The second way to use this list is to ask how one of the items in the picture would be used to help solve the problem. This approach will require the mind to take a huge jump. Where it lands can only be creative.

Recommendations:

1) When a photo is selected, ask the group what the item is and what it does. If it is not clear, ask what it might be. It is not important whether the answer is correct or not. If it initiates new conversation or ideas, go with it. You can always come back to the real item later.

2) You may choose to have someone explain what they know about the item and what thoughts it provokes.

3) It is also important that every element in the photo be used as an idea igniter. If someone picks up a tiny image in the lower corner, let the discussion flow and see where it takes you.

#5 Picture This Prompt List, Numbers 1-30

#1

#2

#3

#4

#5

#6

#7

#8

#9

#10

#11

#12

#13

#14

#15

#16

#17

#18

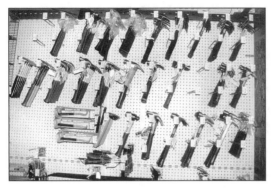

#19

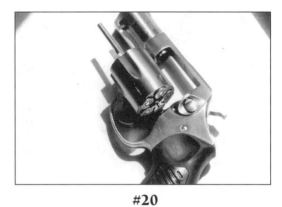

#20

#21

#22

#23

#24

#25

#26

#27

#28

#29

#30

#6 Use Your Senses, Introduction Numbers 1-5

Really creative people tap into everything, but, just like the rest of us, they only have five ways of doing it: touch, sight, sound, taste, smell. No matter how creative someone is, she has no more tools to ignite the imagination than you. The key is to use those tools in such a manner that they help form new images. That is the goal of the Use Your Senses Creative Prompt List.

There is a trick that can help bring out the best from the group when using this list. Most of us rely primarily on three senses for our communications: sight, sound, and touch. Taste and smell are present but to a much lesser degree. In almost everyone, one of the "big three" will predominate. For some, it may be sound. This group will process information more through the sound of the communications than the way it feels or the way it looks. They will respond to prompts like, "Do you hear what I am saying?" "The sound of rain as it hits the street." Visual people will respond to the way something looks and will react to prompts like, "Can you see what I mean?" "Draw a picture to explain what you mean." For the tactile, or touch people you should prompt with, "How do you think that would feel?" or "That's a solid idea."

Watch how individual members of the group respond to sensual prompts. If you see a group member respond in one of these three primary areas, try to tap into that sense when talking to that person. Use a prompt as described earlier if it is pertinent to the discussion. It will take some practice to recognize these modes of communication, but it is worth the effort. If your attempts don't bear fruit at first, don't worry. It won't harm your efforts. Just keep at it and remember: just because someone may be a visual person does not mean he has no auditory or tactile skills. It just means the visual is his primary mode. He will also respond to other sensory inputs or prompts although not quite as strongly.

The strength of this list is its ability to get people thinking with all their senses. If a player has never before thought about how a staff meeting tastes, all the better. Now she is in the realm of the unfamiliar and has more chance of getting new ideas.

Recommendation:

Paint a picture of the sense before handing it over to the group. Each sense has a little introduction you may want to read aloud. Embellish it as you see fit. Give it all the life you can. It will be fun and you'll spark more thinking

It will take some facilitation skills to have people reach beyond their standard response mode into one filled with sensory fancy. Give it a try; you may find you can really get into it.

#6 Use Your Senses Prompt List, Numbers 1-5

1. How would it (the problem and/or its solution) smell?
Imagine the smell of the sea. The salt air. Or a musty basement. A single rose. Onions, garlic, and mushrooms frying in a hot pan. If this problem has an aroma, what would it be and why?

2. How would it look?
The multi-colored sky ablaze with fireworks. Rolling red hills of sand baking in the shimmering heat of the desert. All the colors of a sparkling rainbow. Sunlight filtered through muslin on an azure blue rumpled sheet.

3. How would it taste?
A bitter lemon squeezed in your mouth. The sweet taste of cotton candy. The anticipated taste of chocolate just before you bite into a Hershey Bar. Lipstick.

4. How would it feel?
Hands on skin tracing the contour of a back on a hot humid night. A burlap bag. A new oriental rug on bare feet. The sun baking your oiled body on a sandy beach. Feet digging in beach sand.

5. How would it sound?
The power of a locomotive. In the stillness, a single bird. Rain on the street, like frying bacon. The pounding surf. The roar of a football game. An erotic "yes."

#7 Game Break, Introduction, Numbers 1-30

The object of Game Break is to spark new and potentially outrageous thinking. Use it when ideas start to go stale or whenever your group just needs a break.

The challenges in Game Break are clearly outside the sphere of the problem you are trying to solve. In fact, they are probably outside most people's knowledge, experience, or socially accepted biases. That's OK. There is no requirement to know anything about the subject; that's not the point. Lie. Lying is not only expected, it's encouraged. The bigger the lie, the better. For really imaginative lies, there should be a reward . . . Reese's Peanut Butter Cups are ideal.

As the challenge is being addressed, the group members need to listen with their most creative ears. As the person is talking, wild notions and weirdness will roll around in everyone's head. That's good. Urge people to speak out when that happens, even if the idea is half-baked. Half-baked ideas spark discussion. Go with these ideas and see where they take you. If an idea pertains to the problem, write it on the board for further exploration or refinement.

The strength of the Game Break is as a terrific diversion if you need to recharge the creative batteries or want some off-the-wall options. Nothing here should be serious. Let the wild ideas and fun begin!

Recommendations:

1) Use Game Break when and if things start to get too serious.

2) Use Game Break if ideas start to run dry and the players need to shift gears.

3) Use Game Break just because it's fun.

4) Not everything here has to relate to the problem/objective. If it does—great!

5) If a group seems uptight or self-conscious, Game Break could be just what you need. Be careful, though, because the wildness here could make some players even more self-conscious.

#7 Game Break Prompt List, Numbers 1-30

1. Tell everyone about the time you met Millard Filmore and he told you how much he enjoyed the most recent edition of the Kama Sutra.

2. When you are looking for a pair of new tap-dancing shoes, what requirements do you have and how do you know when these requirements have been met?

3. In only ten words, tell how you change a light bulb. Keep your eyes closed and use lots of hand motions.

4. Explain, in pantomime, how to milk a cow. Start with getting the pail and end with adding chocolate and drinking the milk . . . don't forget about cleaning the udder!

5. Explain what to look for when selecting a prize Hereford bull for breeding . . . be specific.

6. Explain the Theory of Relativity, how it was conceived and how it affects the rising of a soufflé during an eclipse.

7. Explain exactly how socks get dirty, if they get dirtier than undergarments, and why.

8. Pretend you are a tank of gas in a car. Explain the voyage you take to go from the gas station pump to the exhaust pipe, where you are captured by the catalytic converter (give the converter a pet name). Choose someone at the table and have that person explain how the (pet name) works.

9. Explain how a steam engine drives a train. Be specific about the mechanics of steam drive. Explain how the whistle works and hum a tune that only a train whistle can play. Have three other people join you with the humming.

10. Think of three circus performers you feel would be helpful in solving this problem. Explain what talents they have that would make them helpful.

11. Name three fictitious characters that could make this problem worse. How would they do it?

12. Explain, in detail, how flowers reproduce. Refer to specific organs of reproduction.

13. Explain how a company can produce 600 pot pies per minute. Tell how the process works.

14. What questions would you ask Albert Einstein about how to solve this problem? Ask two people to interpret the answer he would give.

15. Assume you know nothing at all about this problem. Ask the group at least three really, really stupid questions. If the questions are not stupid enough, the group can make you ask one more. One of the questions must be asked in another voice, such as a baby or sexy woman.

16. Explain how a vacuum cleaner bag works and why Jello, puppies, and black-eyed peas in fatback should not be sucked up.

17. Cucumbers are soaked in brine to make pickles. What would you soak this problem in to solve it?

18. Using only hand motions, show how peanut butter is made and how to make a sandwich with it and grape jelly.

19. If you had to marry a gorilla, explain the criteria you would use to choose the very best gorilla. How would you explain the relationship to the bellhop at the hotel?

20. For three minutes, have everyone at the table think up the most ridiculous solution to the problem they can. Next, vote on the winner. Everyone has to give him/her a nickel.

21. Explain in exact, excruciating terms what goes through a quarterback's head just before he is tackled by a 320-pound lineman. Explain his thoughts for the ten seconds following the tackle. How would your thoughts be different?

22. If the world was going to end in three hours, and you had to solve this problem to keep that from happening, what would you do?

23. Pretend a solution to this problem is at the center of a dart board. "Less than perfect" answers surround it. Throw a dart that hits one of these "less than perfect" solutions. What does it say?

24. If someone told you that you were really creative except for one thing, what would that one thing be? How would you fix it?

25. Look around the room and find one thing that could be improved. Tell everyone how you would improve it. Make the people at the table add to your idea.

26. Explain the way you would go about damming a small stream so you could generate enough energy to power your house. How would you keep people from skinny-dipping in the pond, and why?

27. How are maps made, who invented them, and why (not just to tell you where you are)? Geez, that's no fun.

28. Why do sinks and toilets get clogged and how do they get unclogged? How would you unclog them without a plumber, plunger, or Drano?

29. If you had in your hand a brand new Ruger SP 101, 357 magnum with 158 grain hollow-point, jacketed bullets and shot into a 25-pound smoked Polish ham, what would happen?

30. Make the problem into a sex symbol and tell why you choose the words and images you did.

PART 6

Walking the Walk: Taking Action

BenBalance

The session has been productive; you have a handful of ideas that may solve your problem. Mission accomplished, right?

Not yet!

Up to this point, you've been instructed not to pass judgment on the ideas that have been generated. Now it's time to examine the ideas to see which ones have merit and how they can be used to solve the problem. This can be tough, particularly if you just know you have *the* breakthrough idea of the century and nothing can stop you. Proceed with an open mind.

The BenBalance, named after Ben Franklin, who used this technique to judge ideas, is a tool to help you look at the pros (+) and the cons (-) of any idea. In the left-hand column of the BenBalance Worksheet (at the end of this section), under "Likes," list everything you/your group likes about your idea. Be sure to list everything. You'll be surprised to find that new thoughts come up that can add strength to the original idea. Note these "new" ideas on a separate pad. They will expose new and unexpected dimensions to what was already a solid idea.

In the right column, under "Dislikes," list all the concerns expressed about the idea. Again, be sure to list them all. Next, "balance" the two lists and see if you have a workable idea. Balancing the points can prove a challenge. Not all points are equal. Analyze each point to determine its relative strength in the equation. For example, you may find there are only one or two items on the minus side, as opposed to five or six on the plus. These two "dislikes" can have more power than all the "likes" and can kill the idea. Try Brainstorming or using The Game to find ways to overcome these concerns. If you can't overcome them, you may have to shelve this idea for now.

The advantage of a BenBalance is that it gets everything out on the table. You'll know what you will be facing when the idea meets the real world. It also makes you ready for the inevitable question, "Yes, but have you thought of . . . " Your answer will be, "Yes, and . . ."

BenBalance Worksheet

IDEA, SOLUTION, OR ACTION

_____

LIKES (+)	**DISLIKES (-)**
1	1
2	2
3	3
4	4
5	5
6	6
7	7
8	8
9	9
10	10

PROJECT NAME _____   DATE _____ PG. _____ OF _____

Specific Actions

You have your idea. You've conducted a BenBalance, and now you're ready to get going. The Specific Action Worksheets are designed to determine the exact actions you'll need to execute your solution. The term "specific" is important, because that's what you must do—be specific.

At the top of Specific Actions Worksheet 2, write your solution. Under Specific Actions, list everything that needs to be done to achieve this solution. Don't worry about the order, you can arrange the actions later.

One way to start this process is to have everyone do a Mindmap of what they see as the necessary actions. List them up on the board. Another method is to try the "double how" technique. This is as simple as asking "how" we will achieve the desired solution (see Specific Actions Worksheet 1). The answer to the first "how" will usually set the stage. The second "how" will focus on the specific actions necessary to reach the solution. If you feel you need a third or a fourth "how," keep going.

Either way, once the actions are listed, arrange them into an appropriate sequence. This can be functional or chronological.

Once you have determined the very specific actions necessary to reach your objective, you'll need to determine what resources you'll need to complete the actions. Move to the next section, Resources, to proceed.

Specific Actions Worksheet 1

HOW HOW TECHNIQUE

How

How

How

How

How

How

SOLUTION

PROJECT NAME _____

DATE _____ PG. _____ OF _____

© FLOYD HURT 1999 1 (800) THINK NU

Specific Actions Worksheet 2

DESIRED SOLUTION

_____

_____

_____

SPECIFIC ACTIONS TO ACHIEVE DESIRED SOLUTION

1 _____

_____

2 _____

_____

3 _____

_____

4 _____

_____

5 _____

_____

6 _____

_____

7 _____

_____

8 _____

_____

9 _____

_____

PROJECT NAME _____   DATE _____ PG. _____ OF _____

Resources

Never end the creative process without filling out the Resources Worksheet. If you are not planning to take an action toward solving the problem, don't spend the time and effort having the meetings . . . unless you just need to "get together."

The Resource Worksheet is designed for one purpose: to execute the solution by assigning specific actions to people and determining the necessary resources to accomplish these actions.

From the Specific Actions Worksheet pages, list the actions required to achieve the solution. In the next box, entitled PERSON, write in the name of the *one* person responsible for overseeing the completion of this action. If an action requires a committee, the name of the chairperson goes in the box . . . not the name of the committee. This will assign ownership of the action to a specific individual and prevent lots of finger pointing later on.

In the MATERIAL REQUIRED box, write in the tools, money, people, room, etc. you will need to execute the action. Be as specific as you can. You may need to refine this at a later meeting but, for now, put your best guess in that box.

In the DATE box, write in the date or time when the action must be completed. This must be an exact date, such as "July 23," not just late July. By having a specific date, you will be able to set milestones for activities that are dependent on each other for completion. A firm date will also let everyone know when they will need to get together again to review progress.

Once the Resources Worksheet is completed, get ready to CELEBRATE. Celebrations should be planned and adhered to. Keep on reading to find out how.

Resources Worksheet

	ACTION	PERSON	MATERIAL REQUIRED	DATE	✔
1.					
2.					
3.					
4.					
5.					
6.					
7.					
8.					
9.					
10.					

PROJECT NAME _____   DATE _____ PG. _____ OF _____

Celebration Document

Feedback is a critical part of solving a problem and getting the job done. You have been assigned an action. How will you know when your action has been completed? This may seem like a simple question, but sometimes the answer is shrouded in confusion. On the Celebration Document the group spells out the exact criteria everyone will use to determine when an action has been completed.

For example, if the action listed was to have a telephone installed, the Criteria for Success would be, "Pick up the phone and make a call." No ambiguity, no "yes, but's," and no misunderstanding about what is expected. The feedback is clear, and the person can now move on to a new challenge.

The reason for calling this a Celebration Document is simple. When an action is completed, celebrate. "Life without celebration is like a gift without wrapping." Bring in some M&M's, order a pizza, or if the challenge is big enough, award a fat bonus. A little celebration goes a long way in keeping everyone charged up . . . use your imagination.

Celebration Document Worksheet

	ACTION	CRITERIA FOR SUCCESS	COMPLETION DATE	✔
1.				
2.				
3.				
4.				
5.				
6.				
7.				
8.				
9.				
10.				

PROJECT NAME _____   DATE _____ PG. _____ OF _____

© FLOYD HURT 1999 1 (800) THINK NU

Sniper Trap

They're out there . . . they lie in ambush and as soon as you present your well-honed idea, they attack. They're ruthless . . . "Ha, we tried that last year." "Yes, but . . ." "Where do you expect to get the money?" "Do you think manufacturing will ever go for such an idea?" They are the "snipers" who sit in the dark clutching their guns—guns loaded with their very strange and very secretive thoughts as ammunition . . . "How come my group didn't think of that?" "That's a feather in their cap, not mine." "This could make me look bad."

That's not all. Sniper shots can come from other, unexpected sources: traffic jams, snow storms, a missed phone call, and a host of other obstacles can send your best intentions into a tailspin. Your job at this stage is to anticipate and intercept or re-direct as many of those potential bullets as you can. It can be a real challenge, so you'll have to bring your best talent to it.

A Sniper-Trap is designed to provide a plan of action if something or someone gets in your way. If this happens, you have one of three courses of action.

- First, you can abandon the plan altogether. That's a dandy action if there was not much value in the idea to begin with. You should know this well before you reach this stage.

- Second, have a preventative plan in your pocket that you can pull out and execute if things start to come unraveled.

- Third is to have a contingency plan that will allow you to come in through another door to accomplish an acceptable (though not necessarily the best) solution.

SNIPER TRAP PROCEDURES

Step 1:

Write the solution to your problem on an easel pad. Post it so everyone can see.

Step 2:

List all the actions that will need to be taken to solve the problem. Take these from the Specific Actions Worksheet.

Step 3:

Take each action separately and have the group list everything that can go wrong (the snipes) with the action as it is stated. This is called Reverse Brainstorming. Be sure to list every Snipe no matter how insignificant it may seem. As the Snipes are presented, discuss the origin of each one. You will need to name names, and be specific about the nature of the Snipe. There is no room here for timidity or ambiguity. For example, if the group thinks that ol' Joe will shoot down the idea, say so and tell why. It will do no good to address ol' Joe after he has his loaded sniper rifle, aimed at the heart of an action step, and shot a hole through it.

Step 4:

Once all the actions and Snipes are listed, review each one to determine if it is likely to happen, and if it presents any real danger. In making these determinations, have everyone place the Snipe on a continuum:

Risk to solution   *Annoyance* — 1 - 2 - 3 - 4 - 5 - 6 - 7 - 8 - 9 - 10   — *Lethal*

Likely to occur   *No* — 1 - 2 - 3 - 4 - 5 - 6 - 7 - 8 - 9 - 10 — *Yes*

The higher the combined score, the more dangerous the Snipe. Narrow the list for each action down to two or three Snipes that have the potential of wreaking havoc on your idea. Write them on another easel pad.

Step 5:

Review the causes of each of these snipes, and Brainstorm actions you can take to prevent them from occurring. As always, be specific about the preventative action. For example, who is in charge, what will it take, and when will we know that this preventative action will need to be taken? Remember, the best way to solve a problem is to take away its cause. That is the core of preventative-action steps.

Step 6:

Assume things fall apart and your preventative actions can't hold back the Snipe, now what? Proceed to your contingency plan. The object is to find a way around the Snipe and still achieve your objective. It may take a little more time, cost a little more money, or reduce the effectiveness of the action, but the contingency plan will at least get the job done.

Start by reviewing the possible Snipe and the preventative action. Next, conduct a What Then session. If ol' Joe does deliver a decisive blow and the preventative action doesn't work, "what then?" Asking this question will force new ideas to keep things on track. Keep asking the "what then" question until you are confident you have a plan to keep things moving—no matter what. As always, enumerate the Specific Actions. What will we do, who will be in charge, and what will we need? With all the unknown factors, it may be difficult to determine an exact time for executing a contingency plan, but a rough estimate should be included.

Now you're ready. You have a great idea, you've weighed the good and bad with a BenBalance, you know it will work. You've looked at the snipes and know how to prevent or overcome them. You even know how to proceed if someone or something drives a stake into the heart of your plan.

You present the idea to the big boss. He says all the right things: "That's great, but did you think about . . . ?" You look him right in the eyes and say, "Yep, and this is what we will do about it." He says: "What if it doesn't work?" You reply: "Then, we will . . ."

You are stellar. He gives you the OK and you head out into the real world, where nothing ever goes wrong.

Sniper Trap Worksheet

Action Step # _____

SNIPES:

What	Who	Why	How	Risk*
1.				
2.				
3.				

PREVENTATIVE ACTION   **CONTINGENCY PLAN**

1. _____

2. _____

3. _____

*Risk to solution Annoyance —1 - 2 - 3 - 4 - 5 - 6 - 7 - 8 - 9 - 10 —Lethal   Likely to occur No — 1 - 2 - 3 - 4 - 5 - 6 - 7 - 8 - 9 - 10 — Yes

PROJECT NAME _____   DATE _____ PG. _____ OF _____

Epilogue

Epilogue

Why is it called Arete?

At the time of this writing, I am designing a new building to house my advertising agency and a few other tenants. The building will be called "Arete."

For almost 11 years, our office has been in a wonderful old three-story house built in the early 1920's. This house is warm, charming, and provides an excellent atmosphere for the work we do. Our business has expanded from just me, to a staff of talented, intelligent, and very creative people. In a few short years we have careened down a path from hand-set type to type at the click of a mouse. This path is littered with the bodies of those who failed to see the need to change or resisted it to the point of their own destruction. It has been an expensive and often confusing path, daily redefining the word "obsolescence." A path where things don't ever wear out, they are simply superseded. A path where the electronics that drive us have assumed a self-generating life of their own, demanding that we expand, enhance, and update them before they ever reach their own maturity. It is a perfect circle with the power to keep us on the tip of the anxiety curve.

A great deal of the hands-on pride that used to go with the job has been lost along the way, and our connection with what we do is often lost in the bowels of a silicon chip. Much has been displaced and a great deal has emerged and is emerging in the process. Moving from our well-worn, womb-like building is not the result of this shift, it is a change I see in the way all of us will think and do business in the coming years.

But why is it called "Arete?"

There is a point of light, there in the dim future. It has no form, carries no information and provides virtually no navigational aid. It has no running lights. There are no green or red markers we can shoot and triangulate to determine our position. It's just a dot.

When we look back to the past, the navigational information that guided us before is receding faster and faster. It's fuzzy with no center on which to fix our bearings. Even if we chance to sight a particular point with our sextant, it stands alone with no companion and is useful only as a memory, not a guide. If there are no markers, there can be no maps, and the markers vanish faster than we can take a fix. It is impossible to make a map that will take us toward the point of light; if indeed that is where we want to go.

But why is it called "Arete"?

In a world without markers, everyone is lost. If markers from the past recede faster than they can be sighted and a point toward the future is abstruse, we are left with only one choice: MAKE OUR OWN MARKERS. This is the core condition that confronts man at the edge of the post-modern world.

"Arete" means "excellence" in Greek. It is the subject in Aristotle's Nicomachean Ethics. It held Plato and Socrates in thrall. It's the stuff of Homer, Virgil, and the Superman of Nietzsche. It is a word that is bigger than all of these men, but it is the word that made them all great.

The building called "Arete" will carry with it the collective memory and color of excellence. But it will not rigidly adhere to that memory as the "only" way. It will provide an open environment where everyone will be expected not to just do their job, but to find excellence in every aspect of what they do. In a building called "Arete," we will each define who we are in the way we act. We will act with excellence, not because the client wants it, or we may lose our job. We will do it because in a world without markers, the act of becoming excellent for its own sake is the only way to create navigational lights along the path ahead. It will help us keep our bearings. Excellence will be an end unto itself, because on a "lay-awake-at-night" level we all know we are dancing just to dance and that the point of light out there is totally unimportant.

Excellence is infectious. It infects everyone close to it with a driving purpose: to be part of something big, something captivating that is its own measure, requiring nothing except itself.

In a world where the responsibility for our brain rests with a moribund educational system or a demeaning media, where our financial future rests with a bankrupt safety net and our leaders fail to lead, embracing instead a make-believe past, "Arete" will be a haven. It will be the place where the creativity discussed in this book is alive, well, flourishing, and adding immeasurably to the wealth of every person who walks through the door.

This is why it is called "Arete." What will you call your building?

APPENDIX A

Sample Sessions

Sample 1: The Pencil — Attribute Listing, Mindmapping, The Game

The following example illustrates how to incorporate a variety of techniques into an Attribute Listing session to solve a problem.

State the Session Objective:

Find three ways to make a pencil more appealing to kids.

List the parts of a pencil:

Mindmap:

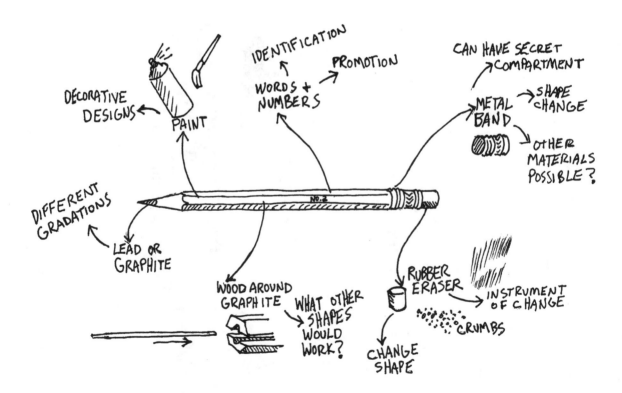

Choose one of the parts for modification

The metal band

Use The Game to generate ideas:

From the Verb Commands List randomly select number . . . 47:

> *"Make it part of something else."*

- What if it could be taken off the pencil and used as a part of a board game? Maybe with a peg that fits in the board. Different pieces fit in different holes. The objective may be to fill a board or collect them.

- It could be made big.

- Punch a hole in it so it hooks in one of the rings of a three ring binder. It won't get lost.

From the Use Your Senses List randomly select number . . . 5:

> *"How would it sound?"*

- Make it into a little radio.

- When you push down on the paper with the eraser, it could give a little chime or play music.

- Make it a beeper.

- Make it larger and turn it into a personal alarm.

From the Heroes List randomly select number . . . 7:

> *"Robin Hood"*

- He could take it off and roll it into a dart for a blow gun. Or make it into a little knife.

- He would make it bigger so he could lift off the eraser and drop in the gold coins he robbed from the rich. The pencils would then be given to the poor . . . like a "learning bank."

- He would make the pencil into a arrow with the band as the feathers. The eraser could be taken off and a message could be placed inside.

Many of these ideas appear to have little initial merit. They will, however, start new thinking. For example, the notion of putting gold coins in the band for the poor may prompt someone to think of poor students. Perhaps a teacher could give a student some kind of a reward for good work. The reward could be placed in the band. When it's full, the student gets a special "gold" pencil. Or maybe there are interchangeable bands of different colors. As a student moves from one level to another, the teacher gives him a new colored band. This color would be a sign of achievement. Every time the student looks at the pencil, he is rewarded.

Keep thinking, you never know where this exercise will take you. Maybe Sherwood Forest.

Sample 2: Big Jim's Grocery — Force-Field Analysis, The Game

Situation Statement:

Big Jim's, a small grocery store, finds itself in a major demographic shift. The younger customers are moving away as a new retirement community is growing into a neighborhood powerhouse.

Problem analysis:

What is?

Big Jim's grocery is losing business due to its current customer base moving out as a new, multi-unit retirement community is opening. Most of the people in the new retirement community have never visited the store and know nothing about it. They still shop at the store in the big mall because "they have always shopped there."

What should be?

A store full of these new retired customers shopping at Big Jim's and spending lots of money on Jim's groceries.

Session Objective:

"Generate at least one idea that can be implemented by our staff that will encourage people from the retirement community to come into Big Jim's grocery."

We are confident that if we can get people to visit the store, they will shop here.

Driving forces (what is currently working for us):

- Near the retirement community.

- Owner is 55 years old.

- Work force of college students nearby could deliver.

- Some people from the community already shop at Big Jim's.

- Store is big and has a good inventory.

Restraining forces (what is holding us back):

- Not a great deal of awareness in the new community of Big Jim's.

- No easy way to get to the store.

- May not have the right product mix.

- People are not accustomed to shopping at Big Jim's.

Most significant forces:

- *Driving:* Some people from the community already shop here.

- *Restraining:* No easy access to the store.

For the purpose of this exercise we will work only with the driving force.

New Objective:

"How to encourage the people already shopping at Big Jim's to bring in other people from the community."

Idea Generation

With this problem posted on the wall, we have a brainstorming session where we use The Game to prompt new thinking. The facilitator chooses to use the Verb Command List. The number 13, "Enclose it" is randomly selected.

The group Brainstorms for a few minutes. These are the ideas presented by the group based on the verb command, "Enclose it."

- Give everybody in the community a paper ring with coupons printed on them. They have to wrap it around a friend's wrist, enclosing it in coupons from Big Jim's.

- Get a big roll of paper, like butcher's paper, wrap it around the building and make a path leading to Big Jim's.

- Have some t-shirts made with the Big Jim logo. These can be given to people who shop at Big Jim's . . . enclose the people who shop there in a t-shirt. They can also be given away by these people to their friends at the community.

- How about a hat? Enclose the head.

- Let's kidnap the people who come to Big Jim's and put them in jail. Enclose them in bars. Make it so their friends will have to come and get them.

After looking at all the ideas, the group chooses:

"Put them in jail and make it so their friends will have to come and get them."

Conduct a BenBalance to test the idea:

Likes:

- Could be fun.

- Will force people into the store.

- Help people get to know each other.

- Could make people pay to get their friends out. Money could be donated for community project.

- Could tie in with "prison" food. Bottled water, really great bread.

Note that some new ideas, donating money for community project and "prison food," came from this part of the process. Big Jim's could have a special on premium bread or imported bottled water. This could be fun and it would help establish the habit of buying something for first-time visitors to the store. Always look for new thoughts during the BenBalance part of the exercise.

Concerns:

- May turn off some people.

- Could be hard to manage.

- Don't have a jail.

So far, so good. It does not appear any of the concerns will negate the idea. If, in your session, the group thinks one point may be a killer, brainstorm ways to overcome it (see Sniper Trap, Part 6). This can keep a worthwhile idea from dying before its time.

Actions:

- Talk to the manager of the retirement community to get approval.

- Talk to people and take photos.

- Make a mock jail.

- Produce a flyer with the pictures of "jailbirds," how to get them out, cost, where money will go, and date.

- Pass out the flyers.

- Hold the event on Saturday, May 22.

The rest of the Force-Field steps (determining Resources, Celebration criteria, and handling Sniper Traps) are filled in on the sample sheets. As you can see, this process got people thinking outside the expected and generated an outside-the-expected promotion at a low cost, which will give Big Jim's valuable visibility and goodwill in the community.

Force-Field Analysis Worksheet *(page 1)*

SITUATION STATEMENT

Generate at least one idea that can be implemented by our staff that will encourage people from retirement community to come into Big Jim's Grocery.

Forces driving this situation toward solution:

Near the retirement community

Owner is 55 years old

Workforce of college students nearby could deliver

Some people from community already shop at Big Jim's

Store is big and has a good inventory.

Forces restraining success in this situation:

Not a great deal of awareness in the new community.

No easy way to get to the store.

May not have the right product mix.

People are not accustomed to shopping at Big Jim's.

PROJECT NAME _Big Jim's Grocery_   DATE _4/10_ PG. _1_ OF _2_

Force-Field Analysis Worksheet *(page 2)*

MOST SIGNIFICANT DRIVING FORCE*

Some people from the community already shop here.

Statement/Objective to strengthen driving force:

How to encourage the people already shopping at Big Jim's to bring in other people from the community.

MOST SIGNIFICANT RESTRAINING FORCE*

No easy access to the store.

Statement/Objective to weaken restraining force:

**Based on estimated return for effort.*

PROJECT NAME *Big Jim's Grocery*   DATE *4/11* PG. *2* OF *2*

127

BenBalance Worksheet

IDEA, SOLUTION, OR ACTION
Big Jim's Jail

LIKES (+)	DISLIKES (−)
1 *Could be fun*	1 *May turn off some people*
2 *Will force people into the store*	2 *Could be hard to manage*
3 *Help people get to know each other*	3 *Don't have a jail*
4 *Could make people pay to get out, donate*	4
5 *Tie in w/ prison food Bread/Water*	5
6	6
7	7
8	8
9	9
10	10

PROJECT NAME *Big Jim's Grocery*   DATE **4/10**   PG. **1** OF **1**

© FLOYD HURT 1999 1 (800) THINK NU

Specific Actions Worksheet 2

DESIRED SOLUTION

How to encourage the people already shopping at Big Jim's to bring in other people from the community.

SPECIFIC ACTIONS TO ACHIEVE DESIRED SOLUTION

1 *Talk to the manager of the retirement community to get approval.*

2 *Talk to people and take photos*

3 *Make a mock jail.*

4 *Produce a flyer w/pictures of "jailbirds". How to get them out. Cost. Where money will go. Date?*

5 *Pass out flyers.*

6 *Hold the event on Saturday, May 24th.*

7

8

9

PROJECT NAME *Big Jim's Grocery*   DATE *4/11* PG. *1* OF *1*

© FLOYD HURT 1999 1 (800) THINK NU

129

Resources Worksheet

	ACTION	PERSON	MATERIAL REQUIRED	DATE	✔
1.	Talk to manager	Bob	Feet to walk to building	Thur. the 15th	
2.	Talk to people and take photos	Julie	Camera, film and about $60.00	Wed. the 28th	
3.	Make a mock jail	Chuck	Cardboard, wood, helper and $150.00	Friday	
4.	Produce and print flyers	Tom	Contact printer, design, print 400 flyers. $232.	Monday the 19th	
5.	Pass out flyers	Ann	Feet	Thur. the 22nd	
6.					
7.					
8.					
9.					
10.					

PROJECT NAME _Big Jim's Grocery_ DATE _4/12_ PG. _1_ OF _1_

Celebration Document Worksheet

	ACTION	CRITERIA FOR SUCCESS	COMPLETION DATE	✔
1.	Talk to manager	Bob will report on meeting	Thursday, the 15th	
2.	Talk to people and take photos	Review results of conversations and look at the photos	Wednesday, the 28th	
3.	Make mock jail	Walk around inside jail	Friday, the 23rd	
4.	Produce and print flyers	Look at and enjoy flyers	Monday, the 19th	
5.	Pass out flyers	At end of day sit around and enjoy ourselves	Thursday, the 22nd	
6.	Hold the event	A lot of people in store	Saturday, the 24th	
7.				
8.				
9.				
10.				

PROJECT NAME 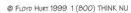 *Big Jim's Grocery*   DATE **4/15** PG. **1** OF **1**

© FLOYD HURT 1999 1 (800) THINK NU

Sniper Trap Worksheet

Action Step # _1_ _Talk to manager of the retirement community_

SNIPES:

	What	Who	Why	How	Risk*
1.	She may not want to get involved	Mgr of ret. comm.	Too much trouble, Liability?	Will say No!	10 – 15 ?
2.	Safety concerns, traffic, heat, too far to walk	Mgr & Police	Getting people across the street	Will not allow it, will not help	12 – 18 ?
3.					

PREVENTATIVE ACTION

1. Explain value to residents and build the "payback" part.
2. Arrange to have "crossing guards"
3. Get police involved.

CONTINGENCY PLAN

1. Go directly to community residents and sell them on idea.
2. Hold the event in the evening when traffic is lighter and it's not so hot.
3.

*Risk to solution Annoyance—1 - 2 - 3 - 4 - 5 - 6 - 7 - 8 - 9 - 10—Lethal   Likely to occur No—1 - 2 - 3 - 4 - 5 - 6 - 7 - 8 - 9 - 10—Yes

PROJECT NAME _Big Jim's Grocery_   DATE _4/15_ PG. _1_ OF _1_

Sniper Trap Worksheet

Action Step # _3_ _Make a mock jail_

SNIPES:

What	Who	Why He won't see value	How He won't make	Risk*
1. No space for Jail	Sam (merchan– diser)	in this	space	14 (8 &6)
2. Too much noise, mess, etc.	The cleaners and check– ers	It will be messy and noisy	They will complain	8 (2 & 6)
3.				

PREVENTATIVE ACTION

1. Have Big Jim talk to Sam
before we make jail.

2. Work after hours and clean
up well.

3.

CONTINGENCY PLAN

Put jail outside and hope for
a sunny day.

Make jail at home and bring
in on Chuck's truck.

*Risk to solution Annoyance —1 - 2 - 3 - 4 - 5 - 6 - 7 - 8 - 9 - 10—Lethal

Likely to occur No—1 - 2 - 3 - 4 - 5 - 6 - 7 - 8 - 9 - 10—Yes

PROJECT NAME _Big Jim's Grocery_   DATE _4/15_ PG. _1_ OF _1_

© FLOYD HURT 1999 1 (800) THINK NU

133

APPENDIX B

The Worksheet Bank

Opportunity Exploratory Session Worksheet

OPPORTUNITY

_____

_____

How did you get the idea? _____

Where were you? _____

Who was with you? _____

Were they part of the idea? _____

How? _____

Will they help you/us refine the idea? _____

What prompted the idea? _____

_____

_____

What are your initial thoughts on how to bring this notion into sharper focus? _____

_____

_____

What do you like about this notion? _____

Concerns? _____

_____

What/who do you need to take this opportunity to the next stage? _____

_____

_____

_____

PROJECT NAME _____   DATE _____ PG. _____ OF _____

Briefing Document Worksheet

PROBLEM STATEMENT/SESSION OBJECTIVE

1. What is the current situation? _____

_____

2. Why is this a problem? _____

_____

3. How did it become a problem? _____

_____

4. Who/what does the problem affect? _____

_____

5. What has been done already to solve the problem? _____

_____

6. What would be the very best possible outcome? _____

_____

7. How will we know when the problem has been solved? _____

_____

8. Are there any similar problems we have faced? _____

_____

9. What are they and what were some of the solutions? _____

_____

_____

_____

_____

_____

PROJECT NAME _____   DATE _____ PG. _____ OF _____

Attribute Listing Worksheet *(page 1)*

PROBLEM STATEMENT/SESSION OBJECTIVE:

_____

_____

_____

_____

_____

ATTRIBUTES OF THE PRODUCT, OBJECT, OR PROBLEM:

1. _____

2. _____

3. _____

4. _____

5. _____

6. _____

7. _____

8. _____

9. _____

10. _____

11. _____

12. _____

13. _____

14. _____

15. _____

PROJECT NAME _____ DATE _____ PG. ____ OF _____

Attribute Listing Worksheet *(page 2)*

ATTRIBUTE FOR MODIFICATION

#_____ _____

Possible Modifications: _____

1. _____

2. _____

3. _____

ATTRIBUTE FOR MODIFICATION

#_____ _____

Possible Modifications: _____

1. _____

2. _____

3. _____

4. _____

ATTRIBUTE FOR MODIFICATION

#_____ _____

Possible Modifications: _____

1. _____

2. _____

3. _____

4. _____

5. _____

PROJECT NAME _____   DATE _____ PG. ____ OF ____

Force-Field Analysis Worksheet *(page 1)*

SITUATION STATEMENT

_____

_____

Forces driving this situation toward solution:

_____

_____

_____

_____

_____

_____

_____

_____

_____

Forces restraining success in this situation:

_____

_____

_____

_____

_____

_____

_____

_____

_____

_____

PROJECT NAME _____   DATE _____ PG. _____ OF _____

Force-Field Analysis Worksheet *(page 2)*

MOST SIGNIFICANT DRIVING FORCE*

_____

_____

_____

_____

Statement/Objective to strengthen driving force:

_____

_____

_____

_____

MOST SIGNIFICANT RESTRAINING FORCE*

_____

_____

_____

_____

Statement/Objective to weaken restraining force:

_____

_____

_____

_____

*Based on estimated return for effort.

BenBalance Worksheet

IDEA, SOLUTION, OR ACTION

_____

LIKES (+)

1 _____

_____

2 _____

_____

3 _____

_____

4 _____

_____

5 _____

_____

6 _____

_____

7 _____

_____

8 _____

_____

9 _____

_____

10 _____

_____

DISLIKES (-)

1 _____

_____

2 _____

_____

3 _____

_____

4 _____

_____

5 _____

_____

6 _____

_____

7 _____

_____

8 _____

_____

9 _____

_____

10 _____

_____

PROJECT NAME _____   DATE _____ PG. ____ OF _____

Specific Actions Worksheet 1

HOW HOW TECHNIQUE

How

How

How

How

How

How

SOLUTION

PROJECT NAME _____   DATE _____ PG. ____ OF ____

© FLOYD HURT 1999 1 (800) THINK NU

Specific Actions Worksheet 2

DESIRED SOLUTION

_____

_____

_____

SPECIFIC ACTIONS TO ACHIEVE DESIRED SOLUTION

1 _____

_____

2 _____

_____

3 _____

_____

4 _____

_____

5 _____

_____

6 _____

_____

7 _____

_____

8 _____

_____

9 _____

_____

PROJECT NAME _____   DATE _____ PG. _____ OF _____

Resources Worksheet

	ACTION	PERSON	MATERIAL REQUIRED	DATE	✔
1.					
2.					
3.					
4.					
5.					
6.					
7.					
8.					
9.					
10.					

PROJECT NAME _____   DATE _____ PG. _____ OF _____

Celebration Document Worksheet

	ACTION	CRITERIA FOR SUCCESS	COMPLETION DATE	✔
1.				
2.				
3.				
4.				
5.				
6.				
7.				
8.				
9.				
10.				

PROJECT NAME _____   DATE _____ PG. _____ OF _____

Sniper Trap Worksheet

Action Step # _____

SNIPES:

What	Who	Why	How	Risk*
1.				
2.				
3.				

CONTINGENCY PLAN

1. _____
2. _____
3. _____

PREVENTATIVE ACTION

1. _____
2. _____
3. _____

*Risk to solution Annoyance— 1 - 2 - 3 - 4 - 5 - 6 - 7 - 8 - 9 - 10 —Leathal   Likely to occur No—1 - 2 - 3 - 4 - 5 - 6 - 7 - 8 - 9 - 10 —Yes

PROJECT NAME _____   DATE _____ PG. _____ OF _____

APPENDIX C

A Creativity Reading List

There are a billion books on creativity. Some are great, some far less than great. Some will be exactly what you need at a given point in your creative development, others will be applicable later. Any list of books will, therefore, be incomplete. The key is to read, think, make notes and come to your own conclusions. In your exploration keep no absolutes. The second you think you've found something that seems absolute, you'll discover a new resource that will override everything. That's exactly the point: keep looking! If you ever believe you've found THE absolute answer, dig a hole, jump in, and close the top; you're done.

1. *Your Creative Power* by Alex Osborn, Charles Scribner's Sons, 1952. This book is the grand-daddy of them all. Osborn was the guy who came up with the term brainstorming and the rules are in this book. It may be difficult to find but it is a great read on the subject.

2. *Applied Imagination* by Alex Osborn, Charles Scribner's Sons, 1953. Published a year after Your Creative Power, this is a great follow-up to it. Although both books are dated, they still contain some great exercises and information. These are foundational books on creativity and should be part of your references.

3. *Serious Creativity* by Edward De Bono, Harper Business, 1992. De Bono is one of the pioneers in creativity thinking. This book offers a broad look at the subject for the serious student. He calls it a "step-by-step approach to creativity on demand" and the book holds up to the sub-title. I find all of De Bono's books helpful but some more than others. This one is among his best.

4. *Creativity* by Mihaly Csikszentmihalyi, Harper Collins, 1996. I love everything Csikszentmihalyi sets down on paper. He is perhaps one of the premier thinkers today. Although a bit more academic than some, this resource offers a solid study in the subject and makes you think in greater detail. This does not mean the book is hard to read, none of his books are, it just means you'll have to spend some time with it.

5. *Flow* by Mihaly Csikszentmihalyi, Harper & Row, 1990. THE book to read about how to enjoy what you do. Although published in 1990 this book can still be found on shelves in most stores. If you have found yourself completely absorbed while doing something interesting, you have experienced Flow. It's a fantastic feeling and this book can help you identify what it is, how to get into it, and what it can do for you.

6. *Creativity and its Cultivation*, edited by Harold Anderson, Harper & Brothers, 1959. This book consists of fifteen articles written by well known authors such as Rollo May and Abraham Maslow. The book is dated but provides some interesting and provocative insight into the creative process.

7. 101 *Creative Problem Solving Techniques* by James Higgins, The New Management Publishing Co., 1994. This is an excellent book for anyone searching for the right technique to use for solving most problems. The book provides quick synopses that almost anyone can use right away.

8. *Techniques of Structured Problem Solving* by Arthur VanGundy, Van Nostrand Reinhold Co, 1981. This is a more complete exploration of actual creative techniques. The book is divided into specific sections such as "Redefining" and "Analyzing Problems to Implementing Ideas." This is a helpful guide in finding which technique to use when.

9. *Mindmapping* by Joyce Wycoff, Berkeley Books, 1991. Published in 1991, this book has become a standard in how to do mindmapping. It is a great way to learn the technique and make it part of your creative thinking.

10. *Conceptual Blockbusting* by James Adams, Addison Wesley, 1974. First published in 1974, this book has been reprinted at least three times. It's a great book that pulls together a wide range of thinking and exercises. I have no idea where the 9 dots notion originated but it is explained and amplified here with provocative results.

11. *Creative Thinking and Brainstorming* by J. Geoffrey Rawlinson, John Wiley & Sons, 1981. This book adds greatly to the understanding of brainstorming and a couple of other techniques. If you can find a copy, it will be help you enhance your ability to set up and conduct brainstorming sessions.

12. *Thinkertoys* by Michael Michalko, Ten Speed Press, 1991. Want more ways to challenge your thinking? This book is exactly what you need. It is chock full of ideas and projects to get your mind going in new directions.

13. *Cracking Creativity* by Michael Michalko, Ten Speed Press, 1998. This is another step in Michalko's ability to take you into new territory. In this book he provides more techniques and ideas on how to kick your brain into unknown territory.

14. *The Young & Rubicam Traveling Creative Workshop* by Hanley Norins, Prentice Hall, 1991. This book hit the shelves in 1991 and is still out there. If your focus is on creativity in advertising and marketing, this book is a must. Not only does it help you understand the creative process, it places it in a context.

There are great numbers of books on philosophy that I would love to recommend. I am aware however, that most of us don't want to tackle the subject. Don't let the word philosophy scare you. It's tough, but there is nothing in the world that will make you think like finding a Baudrillard statement on contemporary society: "we no longer make ruins and relics, we make waste and residue." Think about it.

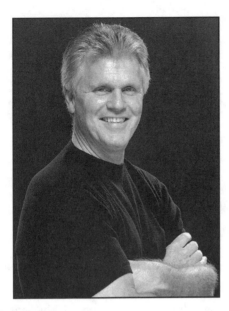

Floyd Hurt

A Serious Student of Creativity

For over three decades Floyd Hurt has passionately pursued the mysteries of creativity not as an academic, but as an "in the trenches," front-line producer. From pounding the streets of New York as a sales rep, to developing and marketing new products for ITT Morton Frozen Foods Division, to founding his own advertising agency, Floyd has earned his "creative wings" in every phase of sales, marketing, and advertising.

Through his work with products as diverse and video programs and fruits pies and organizations as diverse as NASA and PepsiCo, Floyd has amassed a wealth of experience, resources, and understanding which he distills into products, publications and presentations.

In his keynote speeches and other presentations Floyd shares his passion for practical, useful, "life-changing" creative thinking and helps people and organizations achieve real world results like these:

- Personal. professional, and business growth through discovering and capitalizing on NEW opportunities.
- "Out of the expected," productive, profitable NEW ideas.

- Market expanding NEW products and services.
- More clearly focused and effective marketing.
- Stronger teams, better cooperation.
- Better decision making.
- Unique personal insight.

If you are looking for a breakthrough personally or in your work, one of these programs can help you:

- Rousing Creativity: Think New NOW!
- Mastering Your Marketing, Creatively
- Creative Teams, Profitable Results
- Hands-On Creative Techniques

Other products available from Floyd Hurt & Associates:

- *The Benefit Finder*™

A powerful new tool that will revolutionize your marketing and sales efforts. Give this simple, elegant, solid brass, hand-crafted desk accessory to all your staff and prospective clients to get them laser focused on what matters most: How your product or service BENEFITs your customer.

- *Rousing Creativity: Think New NOW!, The Video.*

  50 high impact minutes that will take you all the way to creative action.

- *Rousing Creativity, The Booklets.*

  Ten Steps to Setting Up and Leading a Brainstorming Session

  How to Facilitate a Productive Group Session

  How to be a Member of a Productive/Creative Group

Give us your feedback or find out more:

Floyd Hurt & Associates
1004 East Jefferson Street,
Charlottesville, VA 22902

1-800-Think-NU
FAX: (804) 296-6683
Cellular: (804) 981-5725

www.rousingcreativity.com